ADVENTURES IN MANIFESTING

ADVENTURES IN MANIFESTING

PASSION AND PURPOSE

Sarah Prout and Sean Patrick Simpson

The Adventures In Manifesting series: Volume #3.
First published 2012 by Älska Publishing

Office based in Melbourne, Australia

Typeset in Giovanni LT 9/12/14 pt

© Sarah Prout and Sean Patrick Simpson

The moral rights of the authors have been asserted.

National Library of Australia Cataloguing-in-Publishing entry:

Authors:	Prout, Sarah 1979 – / Simpson, Sean Patrick 1984 –
Title:	Adventures In Manifesting: Passion and Purpose
ISBN:	9780987325907 (pbk)
	9780987325938 (ebook)
Subjects:	Self help, New Age Publications, Inspiration
Dewey Number:	650.1

Cover design by Sarah Prout

Editorial revisions in house

Printed in Hong Kong

Also available in electronic format

*note that grammar and US/UK English is sometimes reflected in each author's preferred writing style.

www.AlskaPublishing.com

Wholesale Discounts
For competitive rates on bulk purchases, please go to www.AlskaPublishing.com

Disclaimer
The material in this publication is of the nature of general comment only and does not represent professional advice. To the maximum extent permitted by the law, the authors and publisher disclaim all responsibility and liability to any person, arising directly or indirectly from any person taking or not taking action based upon the information in this publication.

Älska means to LOVE

(Say it like this: *elsh-ka*)

This book is lovingly dedicated to people that consciously decide to create their own reality.

CONTENTS

Conclusions

GRATITUDE

With the deepest gratitude we would like to thank all of the Älska authors for sharing their incredible and inspiring stories in this book. We would also like to thank our students in the **AdventuresInManifesting.org** community and *you* (the reader) for supporting the Älska vision of Love and Oneness.

From Sean:

The creation of the latest three Adventures in Manifesting books have been an absolutely incredible and inspiring process. My deepest gratitude is with our project manager Mark Rhapsody for all he has done.

To Sarah Prout – you are amazing and I love you. It is such a joy waking up to you each morning and spending our days playing in the fields of Älska Publishing. Living in the now, reminiscing on the past and dreaming about the future with you is amazing.

To Amr and Angel – thank you for your incredible work. To Olivia and Thomas who are a constant reminder *to be the change*. S&D – You're always to be thanked. To Mom and Dad, you guys rock. To my crew, who are always in my heart every single day.

To some of my greatest inspirations I have yet to meet and befriend: Oprah, Ellen, Will Smith, Jim Carrey, and Richard Branson. Thank you for *being* and inspiring the world not just through what you do, but by who you are.

To everyone in my life, my deepest love and gratitude is with you.

From Sarah:

I would like to thank my dad (Mr. A.A Prout) for your love and support. Your kindness and help with the kids is so greatly appreciated – I love you.

To my man, Mr. Sean Patrick Simpson – you're my best friend and I adore you. Your sublime management skills and dedication to the rapid growth of our company and vision is a true inspiration.

Thomas and Olivia, I love you with all my heart. Thank you for being the beautiful souls that you are.

To my friends, family, and soul family (you know who you are) – thanks for your amazing love and support. It means the world to me.

Many thanks to our awesome team behind the scenes here at Älska-Publishing that keep the company running like a well-oiled machine.

Last but not least… our fur babies Cookie LaLa and Merlin Moonman – you really are amazing little souls in dog suits.

INTRODUCTION

Älska

It is with soul-felt gratitude that we would like to welcome you to the *Adventures in Manifesting* series. It has been designed as a source you will continuously enjoy reading when in search of insight, wisdom, and inspiration. The stories are shared from people just like you that are on a wondrous journey of self-discovery.

From a multitude of unique vantage points, these stories demonstrate active examples of inner guidance, connection, faith, and love that have transcended all limitations. Each story has been written with you in mind.

Reading with Your Soul

Our advice to you is that you read with an open heart, an open mind, and absorb the information that sparks your own adventure in manifesting. When reading from a place of wonderment and curiosity, you are bound to find deep resonance. Ask yourself, "What here resonates with me? What inspired action am I being guided to take? What can I learn from this now?"

Allow yourself to find a connection point within each story and within yourself that is right for you.

Your Own Treasure Map

While you will discover truths that each author has found for themselves, you can find in-between the lines your own truths as well. The wonder of this book is that understanding and resonating with certain concepts will happen at different points in your life. So take your time. Keep the book by your bedside table. Pick it up when you feel inspired and follow your inner guidance to the story you're meant to draw from now. Whether you read through it all in one sitting, or piece-by-piece, you will find this a place of inspiration for years to come.

The Mission of Älska

The mission of Älska is to bestow the teachings of love and oneness and proliferate its message throughout the world. Within these two illuminated concepts is the power of vibrancy, creativity, joy, and inspiration. While the mechanisms of metaphysical principles here have been in place since the dawn of time, it is our purest intention to continue this work that began to gain prominence at the beginning of the 19th century in the New Thought Movement.

What are you Manifesting?

You may have noticed on the front cover this very powerful question. Ask yourself this to begin reading with some basic intentions and ideas of what you desire. Just as we would teach you, we are *acting as if* and actively demonstrating how to imprint the Universe with the vibration of success, thus the questions.

In the years before Jim Carrey became a superstar, he wrote himself a check for $10 million dollars and added "for acting services rendered". He carried it in his wallet from that day forth until the abundance and recognition that he desired started to manifest in his life. This act of setting an almighty intention contributed to his success eventually growing to fruition. As witnessed, the Universe responds to what is radiated energetically.

Your Journey Begins Now

Start it from a place of love and gratitude, knowing that as you read you will find resonance with what you are in alignment with in this point of time.

You will find yourself beginning to develop a story through direct experience of your intended reality. As you do, we will be here waiting with expectant joy and an open heart to see what you have to share with the world as well.

Until then, we will look forward to hearing all about your own adventures in manifesting.

With Love and Gratitude,
Älska

About Älska

Älska is the combined energies of Sarah Prout and Sean Patrick Simpson. The company name means *Love* and was received as gentle guidance one evening after a very intense session of laughter and joy.

You say it like this: 'elsh-ka' – which is slightly different than the original Scandinavian pronunciation of their verb (which means *to love*).

Sean and Sarah were prompted from within to start a metaphysical publishing company based on their mutual adoration of Universal truth and passion for writing. Hence, Älska was created!

http://www.alskapublishing.com

THE MANIFESTING COURSE

Get The Manifesting Course and join the Adventures in Manifesting community to connect with other like-minded and inspired individuals:

www.AdventuresInManifesting.org

Share Your Experience

Has a particular story, insight or teaching stood out to you?

We'd love to hear about your experience, so feel free to get in touch and let us know. You can e-mail us at:

feedback@adventuresinmanifesting.org

Additionally, with the intention and desire to share stories and teachings from all walks of life, we'd like to invite you to potentially be a part of one of the next *Adventures in Manifesting* titles.

Stories of all topics about manifesting are welcome (success, spirituality, health, happiness, wealth, love, prosperity, inner guidance, achieving dreams, overcoming obstacles, etc.)

If chosen as a top submission, we will get in touch directly to invite you to be a part of one of our next *Adventures in Manifesting* titles.

Please go to www.AdventuresInManifesting.org to share your experience (not to mention join the course and community, as well as find the hard copy, Kindle and iBook versions of other titles in the series).

Enjoy!

YOU ARE THE ARTIST OF YOUR OWN LIFE

Sarah Prout

I was sixteen years old and a friend dared me to enter the Red Hill Show Girl Beauty Pageant. Not one to back down from a bet, I agreed to win a place in the contest or be forced to eat an entire jar of mayonnaise if I lost the little wager.

My hair was crimped within an inch of its life. I wore a pale blue baby-doll dress, white stockings, and patent leather Mary Janes. My style icon of the mid-1990s was Courtney Love, famous for wearing bright red lipstick and having messy hair and lots of thick black mascara. My intention was to stand out like a sore thumb, make fun of the contest, and miraculously land a winning place.

A man with a microphone was walking down the line of finalists asking us the defining question that would help the judging panel select a winner. He looked like the stereotypical used-car salesman or a game-show host on the brink of retirement.

In his best radio voice he said, "What do you want to be when you grow up?"

There were literally five tall blonde girls that all said they wanted to be *marine biologists*.

It was then my turn to say something.

"I want to be an *artist*," I said.

There was an eerie silence. I was standing on a giant stage in front of a crowd of hundreds of people and I felt like I'd said something so unexpected that it made other people feel slightly awkward.

"And *how* to you intend to make money out of that?" questioned the man.

This was one of those moments in my life that cemented my beliefs about entrepreneurialism.

"My dad has been a professional artist for twenty years," I responded cheerfully.

"Well, hopefully he'll be able to teach you a thing or two," he condescendingly patted my head and went onto the next girl who ironically said she wanted to be a *marine biologist* just like the others.

Surprisingly, I left the Red Hill Show that day with a tiara, a sash, prize money, and a burning desire to make money from living my passion as an artist.

My Belief About Passion

When I was born in 1979, my dad quit his job. You'd think that when a baby is on its way into the world the last thing you would want to do is ditch your financial security and become self-employed. He felt a strong desire to follow his dream and become a full-time artist. Was he crazy? Or was he in beautiful alignment with what would serve him best? It took some serious guts to step out of his comfort zone and believe in his passion enough to provide for his family.

My childhood was spent in galleries, studios, and illustrious exhibition openings surrounded by people that appreciated creativity. What I didn't realize at the time is that my role model for entrepreneurialism was my dad. He lead by example to show me how believing in your own power of creativity will open many doors to many opportunities.

The Sufi poet Rumi once wrote: "Let the beauty of what you love be what you do."

I was so fortunate to have been raised with this philosophy to form my professional compass. I couldn't imagine working in an office for someone else. I feel a great sense of compassion for people that are trapped in the cycle of delayed gratification of living up to their fullest potential as a creative soul.

Time Is of the Essence

I believe that everyone is passionate about something and that life is not a dress rehearsal. So many people live their lives as if happiness is a future destination. In modern society, many believe that they are only allowed to pursue their passions when they retire. Duty comes first and then the love of what they would really like to do. Why have people created rules for themselves where the two worlds of passion and income have to be kept separate?

If you were handed a death sentence today and knew you had only six months left to live, how would you want to spend the rest of your life? Would you look back and see everything as awe-inspiring fulfilment or bleak disappointment?

The concept of lying on your deathbed is so interesting. Pondering one's own exit from this earth plane is really helpful to kick your butt into asking powerful questions that could determine a better future for yourself.

If I was going to die tomorrow how would I spend today? At the end of my life will I see mostly love or regret?

We live in such a busy age where to-do lists are out of control and priorities are all screwed up to the point where we forget to love ourselves and tend to our spiritual development.

Loving yourself is rising above what you think you know and being open to the possibility of something better. Loving yourself is allowing your passions to flourish. Loving yourself is being true to yourself.

How to Define Your True Passion

When you're doing something that you're passionate about, it has the transformative power to make time stand still. You'll be working away at your activity and notice that time flies by so fast. You become all consumed by the joy your true passion gives you that you feel nurtured on a soul level every time you do it.

My partner Sean and I once went to a sushi restaurant in the sunshine coast of Queensland, Australia, called Red Mango Roll to celebrate our anniversary. The Sushi chef was a true artisan with the food he prepared. Every dish was crafted with love, beauty, and thoughtfulness.

3

We could feel that this guy was truly living his passion and the love he had for his work was shinning through in the exquisite way he presented his artwork (the food).

We sat at the table enjoying the colourful array of dishes that were delivered to our table. We'd look over to the chef who was shyly looking to see if we liked his work. We could tell he was getting immense joy from seeing his artwork appreciated. His passion and his purpose were working in unison to deliver an amazing experience for his clients.

To help define your own passions, it's helpful to see how it manifests for others. It's even more helpful to tune into the vibration and the energy of their pursuits. This essence has magical inspirational properties.

Be The Artist of Your Own Life

Being an artist doesn't necessarily mean that you're proficient with a paintbrush. It means you are a creator of meaningful experiences in your life. Everything that you focus your attention to, in conjunction with loving energy... is a creation. Your passion needs to be expressed as a creative outlet. Your passion needs to be let loose, allowed to blossom and freed from the man-made conventions that keep people in mindsets that don't serve them.

The Divine Combination

Passion and purpose are a mutual support system. When you have crystal-clear clarity about what makes your heart sparkle and you can position the activity you love with a profound mission that has purpose, then your world will miraculously transform for the better.

Finding The Right Path

With the profound realization that you are the artist of your own life, you then gain insight into your role as a conscious creator. I believe that your feelings will be your guide in terms of letting you know if you're on the right path to pursuing your ultimate calling in alignment with your passion. However, don't be fooled, every possible path is the right one for it all plays an intricate part in getting your soul where it needs to be guided to. The key is to act from a space of love and the rest will take care of itself.

About the Author

Sarah Prout is the co-founder of Älska Publishing, the *Adventures in Manifesting* series and award-winning entrepreneur. Her bestselling book, *The Power of Influence* has been sold internationally and translated for European distribution.

Sarah's love for metaphysics, design, and business empowerment shines through in her writing, artwork, and teachings. Since 2006, Sarah has built an impressive international media and client portfolio inspiring people to create their own reality.

She reaches over 55,000 followers in over twenty-four countries around the globe with heartfelt, vibrant, and empowering advice about love, business, and style.

http://www.adventuresinmanifesting.org

http://www.sarahprout.com

THE EVOLUTION OF PURPOSE

Sean Patrick Simpson

I was *hellbound* on being a star. There were no if's, and's, or but's about it. It would happen... no matter what. I had my eyes on the prize and I wanted to be famous.

Growing up, I was intricately involved in music. I began playing piano with classical training at the age of eight and singing at ten. All the way through college too I sang my heart out in some of the world's best chamber choirs, a cappella, and vocal jazz groups. My passion was music and I loved being on stage; the blinding lights in my eyes and the wide-open space with nothing but a sea of people in front of me. The roaring sound of the audience was pure bliss.

Combined with my passion for music, I truly believed my purpose was to be a star, whether in the movies, in a band, or as a solo performer.

The Desire to Be Known

Behind the passion for fame, I suppose the real desire could have arisen from a subconscious feeling of insignificance. Since music was what I loved the most, it was natural that the fame was coined up with singing on stage.

Having been home-schooled until 8th grade, I was somewhat sheltered for far too long. I believe it was this life of minimized social interaction compared to *normal* kids that was part of the fuel in my quest for significance. I *craved* connection with others and felt a *need* to be known.

For me, my identity and sense of self became dangerously wrapped up in the idea of being a superstar. I wouldn't settle for anything less.

Sure enough, as my high school years were coming to a close, the bubble I had been living in was getting ready to burst. No longer were my dreams a possibility for *when* I grow up. I *was* grown up. And thus there was an intense discord between what my life looked like *in the now* as compared to what *I wanted* it to.

Without any direction other than to continue on with my passion for music and purpose of fame, I graduated from high school and went on to a junior college with an amazing choral program. There I was able to thrive through the music and friendships I created (though at the same time a large part of me was dying inside through the depression I share more about in *Adventures in Manifesting: Healing from Within*).

My Plan Versus Theirs

At the end of three years when I was ready to move on from junior college and go to a university program, once again I was swept into fear of the unknown. Continuing on to get my music degree was the plan, but it was not *my* plan.

Since high school I could see no point in getting the degree. Sure, it was said that doing so could secure one's future and *guarantee* a better paying job. What a joke! Despite my parents seeing the purpose in a degree though, I did not. I didn't want the jobs this could lead to and had no vision for it.

After transferring to a university for a year and, only having one more to get my music degree, I decided to leave school. "You only have one year left!" my parents argued.

It didn't matter though. I was done trying to fulfill a purpose that was not my own.

Empowerment

Why I left school wasn't just about not seeing any purpose in the degree.

In the years leading up to me leaving school, I had begun experiencing a new passion and potentially new purpose: one that was involved in the fields of personal empowerment. Simply put: In making a difference in the world and for those also in search of meaning.

Within months, I was working with incredible change-makers and world thought-leaders.

My new journey had begun.

I must confess I didn't have a miraculous *a-ha!* of finding a new purpose I was happy with. Amidst the joy and positive states of being, I also had an *immense* sense of inner conflict and dissonance. My childhood crave for stardom was still very much inside me and not releasing its grip easily. The idea came to me that I could earn millions through giving to and empowering people, and then fund my career in becoming a solo performer, movie star, or whatever *in the spotlight idea* I had at the time.

Four years of this push-and-pull continued. I worked in the empowerment field then left it to search more within, bouncing from job to job trying to make ends meet, while embracing whatever lessons I could from my experiences. As I slowly began to mature and release compulsive obsessions of finding significance, I started to experience the meaning I had envisioned helping others find.

Sometimes we find meaning through assisting others in finding their own.

When my love, Sarah, and I came together from across the world, we began to embark on this new journey with one another, finding meaning through service; one that involved creating Älska Publishing, the *Adventures in Manifesting* series, and the empowerment of others.

Now we enjoy together a healthy sense of both significance and meaning.

There Is So Much More

I share this simple story of my journey seeking significance to illustrate a simple point: there is so much more to ones purpose than we may realize.

It is not uncommon to be caught up in *striving* for some kind of purpose, while completely losing the sense of *meaning* in life. Just like anything, striving for a purpose can, if done without consciousness, be unfulfilling.

It's important to know the answer: *in what ways does this purpose add value to both my life and the lives of others?* As without *meaning*, ones purpose can become dangerous. The *something* we are finding purpose or significance in can disappear at the drop of a hat and leave us believing we have nothing.

This disappearance can even happen when the purpose does have meaning, which is why it is crucial to be open to the possibility that one's purpose can morph, transform, or evolve beyond our wildest dreams.

The Balance of Significance and Meaning

It's important to realize that everyone gets significance. There's nothing wrong with it. It comes to people through many ways: accomplishments, parenthood, style, being a part of something, etc.

Some even get it out of claiming insignificance.

By itself however, a search for significance *without* meaning can cause one to become imbalanced and discontent with life as it is; always searching, but never *finding*.

Never *being*.

But when significance is combined with meaning, it can be a grounding force. It can be one that centers and thrusts you into the incredible *now* that is always here and present; a space that can transcend *doing* or *having*, but embraces the two with *being*.

The Choice is Yours

If there was one thing I could give you to take away as you continue finding inspiration in *Adventures in Manifesting*, it would be this: be open to the possibility that there is so much more to your purpose than meets the eye. Whether you have found your purpose, are in the midst of living it, or are finding a new one, consider the possibility that your purpose can evolve and change throughout time. Rather than seeking just to achieve *something*, look within and find where the true meaning is *in* that something, and *then* go for it!

Remember, your passions and purpose in life are for *you* to choose. Others can give you advice. They can even share some ideas or point you in a particular direction. But ultimately, it's *your* choice.

Never settle for anything that is less than what you choose for yourself.

Your life, afterall, is your own symphony. You are the composer. You are the director. And if you live life to the fullest and embrace every step and experience along the way, then no matter how it is traveled, there will be an invisible audience cheering you on every step of the way.

The choice is yours.

About the Author

Sean Patrick Simpson is the co-founder of Älska Publishing and co-creator of the *Adventures in Manifesting* series. He writes and speaks on topics such as mindset, metaphysics, spirituality, business and language patterns.

A musician and singer at heart, Sean has had his compositions played for over 31 million people internationally. You can connect with him and the other authors and readers of this book through the Adventures in Manifesting community.

http://www.adventuresinmanifesting.org

http://www.seanpatricksimpson.com

THE POWER OF PASSION IN YOUR WORK!

Janet Bray Attwood

From the moment I started working at Books Are Fun (BAF), a company that put on book-fairs selling bestselling books at deep discounts in hospitals, corporations, etc, I was a force to be reckoned with!

In my first year there, I became BAF's top sales person and soon broke all of their sales records. By my 4th year there, I had received every award and enjoyed every benefit and luxury that the top sales person in our company of three hundred and fifty employees could enjoy.

I was the queen of the sales department and the perks were incredible!

I loved my job so much, that I even went in on weekends and worked late into the night on the weekdays. I never counted my hours. I was so into what I was doing that I did whatever I thought needed to be done. It was all play to me!

While I was at BAF, the marketing division had their best year ever, and in 1997 BAF became the third largest book buyer in the U.S. after *Simon and Shuster* and *Random House*.

At the end of my 4th year there, the company sold to the mammoth New York based conglomerate, Readers Digest, for a whopping $360 million!

Up until that time, every day was a party. I came into work and left when I wanted to, I got the best territories and the best reps, I had the best office, I went on all of the company's special trips: the world was my oyster. I even made jewellery at my desk in between my sales calls and sold it to the managers of the other departments for a small fortune, and when I got tired of being on the phone, I had a small trampoline and basketball net next to my desk to play with. I even brought my golden retriever to work occasionally. Yup, life was pretty wonderful!

I loved every aspect about my sales job. It was a natural fit for all of my skills, talents, and passions!

At the beginning of my fifth year at BAF, the Vice President of the Company was so impressed with my exemplary sales record, that he asked me to manage the marketing division of forty-five sales reps and also keep half of my sales territory as well to work.

"It's a step up", he said.

Words I would later regret listening to!

Little did I know that what once had been my *ideal career* would soon be the bane of my existence!!

What I hadn't realized when I said *yes* to managing the marketing department, was that I had *zero* passion when it came to managing the sales books, handling all of the complaints, firing and hiring the employees, and keeping all of the sales records in order.

Immediately after beginning the managerial position, the complaints from my reps in the field came tumbling in. They complained to my VP that my attention on them was not what it used to be. Unfortunately I found out, none too soon, that if I put too much attention on managing the marketing department, then my reps in the field were unhappy and complained, and if I put too much attention on my territories, the sales force would be in my VP's office, telling him what a bad manager I was and that I wasn't taking care of their needs. For the first time in years, the passion for my job was gone, and I was miserable!

In my last year at BAF, I earned less, worked longer hours, had a million more headaches, and had a lot less fun. On top of that, the company lost their star sales person!

I knew what had happened.

I had lost my passion.

Finally, and not soon enough, I handed in my resignation.

I believe that in every moment life is a gift. The *pearl* in that moment in my life was that I was able to witness firsthand what it felt like to be in flow; doing what I loved, and being out of flow; doing what I absolutely abhorred.

I witnessed firsthand that when I was doing the work I loved, I became a passionate magnet, I was on the *do less; accomplish more* path where all of the people, the places, and the things that I needed in order to be the best that I could be showed up. And the moment I was doing things that I was not passionate about, not skilled in, not knowledgeable about, the support from the seen and unseen that were usually there, were now no where to be found. My work became a struggle and it in turn affected every aspect of my life.

What You Love and God's Will For You is One and the Same

I learned that the Universe is benevolent and that when life is a struggle, that's the benevolence of the Universe, the gift, of asking us to notice. Notice that we are out of alignment with what our flow is so that we can get back, re-align our selves (so our path is more effortless), *do less; accomplish more,* a path of least resistance; a path of passion.

One of my great mentors, Maharishi Mahesh Yogi, said, "Life is here to enjoy!"

I believe this to be true. So, to be on the path of least resistance.

Here is a question, compliments of my dear friend, Steve Farber, that can help you to get more aligned in your life right now: the question is simply this: "are you doing what you love in the service of people who love what you do?"

Remember: What you love and God's will for you is one and the same.

Enjoy!

About the Author

Janet Bray Attwood is the co-author of the New York Times Bestseller, The Passion Test: The Effortless Path To Discovering your life Purpose, and co-author of From Sad to Glad: 7 Steps to Facing Change with Love and Power.

As an expert on what it takes to live a passionate life, she has shared the stage with, The Dalai Lama, Sir Richard Branson, Jack Canfield, Lisa Nichols and other top transformational leaders.

http://www.janetattwood.com.

WHAT ARE YOU GOING TO DO NEXT?

Nathan Ryu

Do you take the time to wonder why things occur the way they do and what is it all for?

I find that life is an amazing orchestra of experiences; an infinite variation of dimensional occurrences all dancing within each and every moment; moments in which are created for you to experience, learn, apply, and evolve from. These experiences are all for you and all for everyone.

Life's a journey of choices and consequences.

We all have purpose. Just speak to anyone who has found theirs and ask them what is at the core of what drives them to continue on their path to purpose. Some look for it while many don't. Those that find it and live it have the ability to move mountains, big or small.

Like many people, I had learnt during childhood that life can be really tough; it's just the way it is. Not any more special than any-one else, I questioned everything which didn't feel right. I sought my own experiences and lessons until the answers felt right and the outcomes simply worked. I have experienced much pain, lost many things close to my heart, made more mistakes than most, and what wonderful lessons have all these become to accounting to the person I am today.

As you read the various chapters within this book, take some time to write down the answers to the following questions and, while you read, think about how you can create the change you seek in your life.

What are you passionate about? *What* are you actually doing with your life? Is it fulfilling? Did you *really* choose to be doing what you're doing, or are you living your life as a consequence of events and circumstances? Who is *really* in control of your life and future? What is your heart telling you? Have you found your purpose?

What are you going to do next?

I might not share anything new with any of you within this chapter, but my message is simple and has worked for me. I have found that life is simply an experience of constant learning which offers you opportunities to apply these new lessons within. My life has led me to experiencing many things our world has to offer, such as representing Australia in athletics, living life with a beautiful family and group of friends, and becoming a business owner and CEO of the Education Institute. Much of my life's successes and fulfillments are but a direct outcome from living life with two key elements in each and every moment: *passion and purpose.*

When I was eight years old I heard a statistic which asserts that on average, humans only use 10% of their brain capacity. This leads to the obvious question: What is our true potential?

As I saw the light bulb switch on, right there and then the seeds were planted for the journey of discovery called *Nathan's life*. At the age of eight, I already knew that we are capable of great achievements, only by using a small fraction of our potential. The questions of my child hood were: What else are we capable of? What do we not know about how amazing we can be? How is it possible to discover these new opportunities within ourselves?

At the age of eight, it was this moment which I found some purpose and I commenced my Indiana Jones quest to venture the depths of the human experience to discover the greatness which sits dormant within us all.

After the many years of searching the unforgiving rabbit hole warrens, I was ultimately searching for more human capacity percentages equating to a new potentiality in life experience. I found it wasn't until I looked back at from where I had come to where I was at the time, when I noticed some progressive growth patterns. It was a simple confirmation that if one wants to excel in new and amazing ways then it simply boils down to a decision of intent and action.

I discovered through my life experiences that we are significantly more than what most humans understand to date, and that is why I have curiously continued to seek more truth on the mechanics of life and how we all fit into this grand design. To commence, all you need to do is look beyond your own nose and be open enough to what you will find. And you need to do this before having the opportunity to avoid or deny it. After all, you are far more than what you believe you are. Simply find the right people to guide you on your path and enjoy the ride.

Since watching the Moscow Olympics when I was four, my childhood and teenage dream was to compete for Australia. During my many years of being dedicated towards athletics, I found that there were some key elements to being successful: know your twelve-month plan ahead, be the best you can be in each and every moment, and don't *just* believe: *know* you can.

I was used to working with plans, goals, and self-affirming positive messages. When I left the athletics world behind, all I did was take the principles I learnt to be successful within athletics to a career, and found the principles of success were *exactly* the same. It was how my career took off in my early twenties.

At the beginning of each year, I would look back at my previous year to see what I could learn and would proceed to create my plan, goals, and affirmations for the year ahead. Be careful what you wish for; you just might get it. Each morning when I drove to work, I would read out loud the affirmations which were stuck behind my sun visor in the car until they felt like they had sunk into my humanness. While I read them, I also visualized scenarios which in some way symbolized the achievement of these affirming goals. I had been doing this every day for years, and every year I would achieve up to 80% of my goals.

When I was twenty-five, every day I would use multiple types of affirmations depending on what I felt. The following one was an ongoing affirmation I enjoyed working with as the majority of it dealt with how I wanted to feel more about myself: *I love myself, I love who I am, I love who I am becoming, I am financially independent, I am confident and I can do anything.* It was the *I can do anything* affirmation and visualization which nearly led me to my death. As an immature and naive twenty-five year-old manifester, every day I visualized a car hitting me on the road and *it* bouncing off me, which I associated with *I can do anything.* Other than having an extremely healthy and arrogant ego, I am not sure why I created this visualization as I could have created anything to associate with this affirmation.

One normal sunny day while walking to a business appointment in Perth, Australia, I walked across the very same road I did every day for the previous few years. I always checked for oncoming traffic and did so too that same day, but from nowhere, there it was. Everything seemed to slow down within that one moment. I remember, the car hitting and shattering my right leg, and thinking, "Am I being hit by a car? No I'm not." This was followed by my head and shoulder breaking through the windscreen and thinking, "I just got hit by a car! No I didn't!" Then, mid-air while being thrown ten meters from the car, I thought, "Did I just get hit? No, no I didn't."

I wasn't conscious when I hit the ground. But during the time I was unconscious, I found myself in that place: you know, the one with all that bright light and stuff. Standing in the presence of something or someone which I still don't know, I was surrounded by the most indescribable brilliant white light. All I remember is that I had a choice; a choice to live or die. Mine was the former as I still had great things to achieve and so it was from this very moment that my life accelerated towards finding more passion and purpose.

At the end of 2001, and within a matter of six months of the accident, I decided to leave my family, friends, and everything in my life behind and move to Melbourne to create a new life. At that time, I found myself suffering from post traumatic stress disorder (PTSD) from the car accident all while breaking up with my fiancé in a new city in which I had no family support. While dealing with the depths of PTSD hell, I knew I had to stay in Melbourne. I didn't know *why*. I just simply knew I had to.

At the beginning of 2001, I had been working in corporate environments in various roles for years. I was financially comfortable as my career path was set out before me and I had the potential to take it anywhere in any country. And it follows that it didn't make logical sense to look for a career change, so to speak. At the beginning of every year, I was creating my goals and affirmations for the year. One of those goals, one that would fulfil a deep passion I had, was to find a job which would help me work with people to help them improve their lives.

While still suffering from PTSD, it was at that time in which I had hit rock bottom but was looking for direction from within my heart. My passion had always been finding more potential within the human experience and assisting anyone to evolve from it. Consequently, by only following my gut feeling, I found myself working within the Vocational Education & Training (VET) sector.

Here it was: My passion and purpose had come together in balance while my heart was truly singing to see individuals move beyond where they were before they had met us. Ten years on, it was (and still is) the positive changes in our students' lives which has driven us in working hard and inspiring others to step forward into new territory.

It's now 2012. I have more passion and purpose than ever before. I have recently gotten married and our first child is on its way. Like most parents, we want a better life for our children. I didn't particularly enjoy school due to the poor teaching techniques which are still implemented today; I have found that so much human potential gets wasted as a consequence of an educational system which is only catered for the minority. Imagine for a second a school system which doesn't leave any child behind no matter of their financial status, their I.Q, or how stable their self-esteem is; a system which teaches children with *their* particular learning style; a system which teaches our children *how* to actually use their brain and how to deal with feelings and emotions. Imagine an education system which creates a significantly higher outcome in student averages across all socio economics throughout the world.

I am thirty-six years old and still have a lot of great things to achieve. One of my passions and purposes is to work with world educational leaders to create a better tomorrow for our children through constantly improving our worldwide educational systems.

Passions and purposes can be small or large. However, they all amount up to creating a better world.

So, what are you going to do next?

I hope my message as well as this book helps you find that which you are looking for.

About the Author

Nathan is the CEO of the Education Institute and a loving family member. He has many beautiful people in his life, and feels that his role in it is to help others unlock their potential and provide them with opportunities to learn how to achieve more out of life. Nathan wakes up each morning knowing that today his business is going to help others develop a better life through education.

In a time when there is still much pain in the world, Nathan, like many people, feels there is much more life fulfillment ahead of us all.

http://www.educationinstitute.edu.au

SEE, BELIEVE, ACHIEVE

Kelly Salinovich

I always knew I would be successful in life. I also knew that I would be the one to determine the measuring stick for what I deemed to be successful for me. I never bought into materialist success. To me, success always meant having a happy marriage, healthy children, and close and meaningful relationships with family and friends. I didn't care what I materially owned or where I lived. As long as I had happiness with those who meant a lot to me, I would be living a successful life.

I also never believed in measuring my success against others. I believe that everyone has his or her own version of success. Unfortunately, I found that on many occasions, others would compare themselves to me, often branding me as *lucky*. This used to rattle me, but not anymore.

Although to the outside world it appeared that things came easily to me, in my eyes, it was never a case of good luck. I knew it was the result of extremely detailed, well-manifested planning, unstoppable determination, and hard work!

From a young age, even before I was a teenager, I had goals. Lots of them. My goals were not just scribbled down in the boundless way youth may jot down their dreams, they were specific to what I wanted and both measurable and attainable. Even then, I knew without out a slither of doubt, that I would achieve my life goals.

My strong belief in the achievement of my goals was based on the fact that I could literally see it. I could, and still can, see every dream, every desire, and every goal I set for myself in a clear, bright 3D resolution image, like a flawless film flickering in my mind. I vividly imagine myself succeeding in my goals. The images are so real that I can smell, taste, breathe, and feel them.

The moment I conceive an idea of what I want in my mind, I create it. Whether it is career goals, extra wealth, family happiness, or renovating a house, the second that image is burned into my mind's eye, I subconsciously seek out to own it. I make it happen. I don't stop until it's out of my mind and surrounding me in reality. What's amazing is that I also know that *everyone* has this power to think, feel, create, and generate his or her own success – and that even means you.

Perhaps you may feel you are not quite a visual person. Maybe words, pictures of places you want to travel to, or careers you want to aspire to reach are not easily visualized. Other means can be used, such as meditation, voice recording your goals with target dates, drawing a flow chart of the steps to reach your goal, or creating an image board of pictures representing your goals. Find a style that works for you and learn to make it yours. Use your own natural gifts to work for you and help you manifest your dreams into a very attainable reality.

When learning to harness your self-worth and self-belief, take time to observe a child. You will see a child lives in the present moment recognizing and utilizing his or her own talents – sometimes even bragging about it. Children tell us how great they are about *everything*. So why do we lose this in adulthood? Why do we not recognize and take pride in our strengths and abilities? Why do we feel shame and embarrassment in talking about our achievements, but have no problem in laughing about and pointing out our flaws?

Even our so-called *flaws* can be improved or changed into strengths if we desire. My daughter is desperate to be a famous singer. Her dream is to win on The X Factor television show. She is quick to tell people how amazing she is in her strengths, as well as being realistic about her shortcomings. All this without letting her *flaws* hinder the realization of her dreams. Recently, she said to me, "Mom, I know I am going to be a singer and win The X Factor when I am fourteen, but I am not really that good at singing and think I need some lessons."

My daughter is six.

Clearly she inherited my ability to set and manifest her dreams at a young age with sheer confidence. Although I have discovered that this is not necessarily a common trait to possess, it is certainly a trait that can be learned. This is what I do on a daily basis as a spiritual counselor and hypnotherapist.

I strip back years of self-doubt to reveal who my clients are at their core. Everything is uncovered: weaknesses and strengths. I then teach them how to embrace all that they are and all that they can be. I teach them to listen to the only voice in their life that truly matters: their own. If everyone who heard a put-down thought to themselves, *that's a load of rubbish; I am amazing,* then imagine how healthy our mental health and how positive our social interactions with other people would be.

It is upon this philosophy that I have found my true purpose in life. Believe it or not, I had achieved all the life goals I ever wanted for my entire life, just before my 29th birthday! It was a very surreal feeling for me.

Don't get me wrong, I am actually a very relaxed person and cope with change extremely well. Just because I have strong life goals and visions, doesn't mean I am an uptight control freak who falls apart if the script is changed. I roll with the circumstances of life and take it as an inspiration for putting me on the path of success. While I am proud of my successes, I am also grateful. After each success, I establish new dreams and passions, and the process continues.

Since I am well-established in visualization and manifestation, I have also been able to master meditation, which I used to find the path of my next journey.

Besides being a mother, a wife, and a friend, I was in search of my true calling in life. Manifesting my goals was great, but I now wanted to know what my life's purpose was.

Whilst meditating, it occurred to me that *I am here to help others and to write. I am a natural healer and a writer.* With this now secure in my mind, I set off to visualize what I thought a successful healer and writer looked like. Now this has manifested and here I am sharing my strengths with you!

I knew I was a natural healer, but to me, a successful healer was one who was certified. I wanted to create a business of healing people, and in order to do that successfully, in my own mind, I needed to become a qualified and popular Reiki practitioner. I set this as a goal, visualized it, and manifested it.

The true key to success in this life is to make things happen for yourself that are important to you. I have never been one for sitting around waiting for opportunities to fall into my lap. When I've wanted something passionately, I have always put myself out there, accepting the risk of rejection, and created my own success. I am so driven that I even proposed to my husband!

After all, I never wanted to look back on my life and say, "What if?"

It's amazing how your world opens up when you decide to create your own possibilities. It's like when you choose to buy a new car. All of a sudden you start to see that same car *everywhere*! Well, the same occurs with any goal or want.

As soon as you set the wheels in motion towards your goal, your vision expands and you start to notice lots of opportunities right in front of you. It could be an ad in the paper, a song on the radio, a chance meeting with an old friend, whatever it is, if you have your goal firmly visualized in your mind it will be manifested. You will naturally start to become aware of all the opportunities and significant information you need on your path of success.

This happened to me on my Reiki journey. I remember excitedly calling my husband to tell him I had found a course in Perth and flights which lined up perfectly. (I was living in the Pilbara, Western Australia, at the time; not too many Reiki schools there.)

As I was still on the phone with my husband, my young son brought in the local newspaper to me. I thanked him and almost instantly put it to the side, as I rarely had time to read them then. After I hung up the phone with my husband, I subconsciously reached for the newspaper as I thought there may be some advertised flight deals. There weren't, but there was an advertisement from a well-known Reiki master and teacher who was available for sessions and lessons in my town. Thank you, Universe!

Or should I say, thank you me?

After all, if I hadn't have set the wheels in motion, then I probably wouldn't have been looking for discounted airfares in my local paper. I probably wouldn't have opened the newspaper at all! With my goals clearly set in my mind, my eyes were naturally open to all opportunities that life had to offer.

Visualization activated the Universe to respond to my desire.

Obviously, I never boarded the flight to Perth. Instead, I learned my craft in my own town with the most amazing teacher. He had an insane amount of belief in my abilities, and through his teachings, I quickly opened up my spiritual channels into becoming a Reiki Master. This is how my business began as a successful and certified natural healer! Now I was on my way to being a writer.

I sent off my first completed manuscript to a few publishers and was politely turned down. Knowing that failure is just a state of mind and not a point of view, I didn't see this as a failure. Believing in myself and being courageous enough to put myself out there was a process on my road to success and manifestation.

Writing is a competitive field, and when chasing your dreams you still need to have some concept of reality in mind. While another writer may have possessed something I didn't, it doesn't mean I had nothing to offer in the field of writing. I kept everything relative and in perspective. Falling into the trap of self-loathing and losing self-belief is not part of who I am. I knew that opportunities would present themselves and the very real possibility of success was near.

As it turned out, one night I was up late and just started writing these short humorous pieces about human behavior. I had only written novels, poetry, and children's stories in the past, so this was new to me. In my late night delirium I thought to myself, these would make an awesome newspaper column! So I opened up my local newspaper, found the editor's e-mail address, wrote a cover letter, attached a couple of sample column pieces, and pressed *send*. What did I have to lose?

I ended up writing a weekly column for twenty weeks in the Pilbara News and loved every second of it.

There it was. I manifested my goal to become a writer.

Currently I am living my purpose as a successful Reiki and meditation master, hypnotherapist, and corporate health advisor. Through this book, I am also living my purpose as a writer. I haven't even been to Perth for five months since relocating from the Pilbara, and, already, I have established a successful business here. Simple advertising allowed me to gain a loyal client base. Not only did advertising lead me to new and exciting clients, but it also lead to my invitation to write for this book.

Lucky again? Maybe. But after reading this, I am hoping you can see the difference between visualization and manifestation and the term *lucky*.

About the Author

Kelly Salinovich is a happily married mother of two. She has always followed her passions and has become highly skilled and qualified in many things, including being a secondary English teacher, civil marriage celebrant, and, of course, a writer.

Kelly runs her own business and practices as a hypnotherapist, Reiki master, spiritual counselor/life coach, and corporate health advisor. Healing others and helping them grow spiritually and personally is Kelly's life purpose.

Kelly spent a decade living and working in the Pilbara, Western Australia. During this time, she honed her skills working with and helping people adjust and cope with remote country living. Kelly also developed a strong understanding of workplace health issues and recognized a need for a different range of health solutions for employees. Kelly has developed motivational, stress reduction, and positive team building workshops that she delivers to her corporate clients.

http://www.take5healthsolutions.com

HOW FINDING YOUR PASSION CHANGES EVERYTHING

Nadia Flowers

It was Wednesday 23rd of February 2011, the morning after the Christchurch earthquake – a magnitude 6.3. Christchurch city had been devastated. Initial television pictures showed bloodied people being helped along city streets by rescuers. News reports told of multiple fatalities, serious injuries, collapsed buildings, and buckled roads. Urban search and rescue teams had worked through the night to free people trapped in buildings whilst many more remained buried or missing. Christchurch's Cathedral, a historical landmark, had crumbled. We heard that aftershocks continued to rock the city and giant plumes of smoke and dust clouds hung in the air. Traffic jammed as people tried to flee the city in their cars. There were no spare ambulances, no power, no running water.

It was scarcely believable.

In Wellington, I felt quite removed from the devastation of what was unfolding just a few hundred kilometres away. I was early for work; enough to stop at a nearby cafe for a proper coffee. I was feeling excited at the prospect of having some quality time to myself. Thirty minutes of quality quiet, coffee, and immersing myself in my book.

I had a desk job in the Defence Force; a job that really wasn't me. I was very grateful to have it, but each day my spark got a little dimmer as I pretended I was satisfied and fulfilled. I loved helping my colleagues do their job well, but deep down I knew there was something missing. I longed to make a bigger difference, to create something I could call my own; something that was worthwhile enough that I would throw my hat over the wall and go after it with wild abandon for the rest of my life.

Some days I thought this was an unobtainable, selfish, and ridiculous day dream. I also doubted I could do it. After all, I had no degree; no formal business experience and a history of loads of great ideas with little or no follow through.

I had a whole catalogue of notebooks filled with random scribbled ideas which I thought could work or that I hoped I would grow to love. I was relieved to read once that Richard Branson does the same thing and has a whole library of 1B4 notebooks.

Over the years, I had completed many exercises to find my *sweet spot* – that place where talent, passion and ability to actually make a living collide – all with no concrete outcome. My husband and I had slept with giant post-it notes on our ceiling covered with questions. We woke up to *what would I love to do that people would love to pay me for?* each day while I undertook personal profiling assessments to try and gain a sense of my natural strengths and talents. I was longing for some clear direction, something to help me find the thing I would love doing, and the conviction to stick with it.

At the cafe I enthusiastically read my latest book and worked my way through the exercises. As instructed I diligently brainstormed a list of *passions* by completing the sentence *when my life is ideal I am....* Out flowed a list of things that were important to me. Some were material things (things I wanted to have) and some were personality traits or ways of being which I aspired to. Many of the things on my list were things that I wanted to do like *work with a group of inspiring, committed and extraordinary people who make things happen.* Some I already knew and had been consciously working towards and others like *I am expansive, frisky and eager* caught me completely by surprise.

Then, as the book directed one at a time I compared each sentence to the next and ranked my list of passions in order of which was more important.

Then, just like that, my five core passions were revealed. There they were, in black and white. After seventeen years of unsuccessfully searching for meaning, for a true purpose, a definite passion, a clear path, there it was staring right at me. A simple paragraph which completely and accurately captured who I was (and who I still am today). It was both mind blowing and jaw dropping.

Still excited and reeling slightly from finally finding myself I headed to the car and drove to work. I had hardly got through the door when a colleague pulled me aside. It was all hands on deck; all available personnel were required.

In the early hours of that morning, hundreds of people had been evacuated from Christchurch via a RNZAF C-130 Hercules aircraft and a second was on its way. The planes were arriving into Wellington Airport and being met by buses. The evacuees included Australian citizens who had been processed at the newly set up welfare centre down town and had nowhere to go. I was handed a spreadsheet that contained a long list of names with dates of birth and passport numbers alongside. My brief was to do whatever it took to make sure that the people on my list were looked after. The priority was to help facilitate people to get in touch with their families to let them know they were safe. Also to arrange accommodation, emergency passports, and eventually a safe passage back home to Australia.

Before I headed out, I rung several hotels and block-booked as many rooms as I could. After every single hotel room in Wellington was booked, we managed to convince staff at one hotel to turn their beautiful ballroom into a make-shift dormitory. We literally had no idea how many hundreds of people would be arriving.

I jumped into a taxi and headed to the hotel. Evacuees had slowly begun to arrive at the hotel from the welfare centre.

Six hundred specialist doctors and nurses had been attending an international urology conference in Christchurch when the earthquake struck. It was lunchtime and they had run from the dining room in only what they were wearing. Most with no mobile phones, no passports, no coats, no wallets. They had spent a long night huddled under tarpaulins in the rain in a central city park out in the open where debris from further after shocks couldn't fall on them. They had seen bodies lying under bricks and people crushed in parked cars when building facades had collapsed. They were tired, distressed, and dishevelled.

As I checked in with these people and inquired about their immediate needs, it became apparent that some were reacting to their experience. Some were rude and irrational; others were unbelievably generous and helpful. A group of nine who had been together all night absolutely refused to be separated from each other despite having been strangers less than a day earlier. They insisted on squeezing into a standard hotel room and wanted to sleep together on the floor. One girl felt imaginary after shocks and every so often would run screaming from the room.

All day a New Zealand Defence Force Boeing flew back and forward creating an air bridge between Christchurch and Wellington. And all day people arrived at the welfare centre and then the hotel exhausted and desperate.

In a matter of hours I'd gone from frustrated desk bound administrator with a dream of making a difference to working in an emergency situation responding to a never-ending stream of urgent and genuine needs.

After contacting their families, the overwhelming need was to secure passports and flights back home to Australia. Emotions were running high, people were tired, and they wanted answers: when will I get my passport? How can I get a flight home? How soon can we get on a plane? Can I go back to Christchurch to catch my original flight (I just want to go home)? Who will pay the hotel bill? What about my precious laptop with nine half written chapters of my latest book in my hotel in Christchurch? When will I get *that* back? And many more.

An anxious crowd was gathering in the corridor demanding answers. Suddenly something took over; in a loud measured voice I made an announcement. It was strange to hear myself confidently and honestly answering their questions. I told them what I did know and gave my best estimates for what I wasn't sure about. I calmly told them I would provide further corridor updates on the hour. I suggested that each room should elect a key contact person and that I'd liaise with that person until every single person had a passport and a flight back to Australia. It was surprising to hear myself speaking with such clarity and control. Up until then, the only announcement I had made was to my family of four to let them know that dinner was on the table.

With a clear purpose and a sudden and almost unnatural ability to make things happen, I proceeded to do exactly what I said I would do. Somehow after multiple attempts to call Air New Zealand, I managed to get hold of a personal mobile phone number for one of its staff members. With another anxious crowd gathering I explained our situation and begged her not to put the phone down until she had made a booking for everyone. One at a time she painstakingly booked them all, accommodating all of the *not wanting to be separated* quirky and traumatized requests.

When we were done, it felt like we'd caused a miracle.

It wasn't until around 2 a.m. before I was completely finished. I hadn't eaten anything since I arrived at work that morning; I had barely even had anything to drink. I had been operating on adrenalin... and maybe just a bit of passion and purpose.

On the drive home I reflected on my day and remembered that it had all started with me hanging out in a café excitedly uncovering my passions. My number one passion had been very clear: "I am making a difference to large numbers of people, sharing my talents and gifts, and helping them get what they want and need." Wow, who could have predicted the stream of events that followed so immediately after declaring that?

I felt a satisfied exhaustion begin to creep in. I had completely thrown my hat over the wall; I had given myself fully to something. I felt fully used up and it felt glorious. I had done everything I could and more importantly I had become someone I had always wanted to be. I had emerged as someone who could lead, someone who made a difference, and, most surprisingly of all, for someone who had panicked regularly. I had emerged as someone who could keep cool and think clearly under pressure. It brought to mind a bumper sticker I'd seen once: "Life's journey is not to arrive at the grave safely in a well-preserved body, but rather to skid in sideways, totally worn out, shouting... 'holy shit, what a ride!!'"

I had certainly been on a ride.

Goethe puts his thoughts a bit more eloquently:

> "Concerning all acts of initiative (and creation), there is one elementary truth that ignorance of which kills countless ideas and splendid plans: that the moment one definitely commits oneself, then Providence moves too. All sorts of things occur to help one that would never otherwise have occurred. A whole stream of events issues from the decision, raising in one's favour all manner of unforeseen incidents and meetings and material assistance, which no man could have dreamed would have come his way."

I firmly believe incredible things happen when you discover what's truly important to you and then align yourself with it. Clarity and a slight turn in the direction is all that is needed to move mountains.

About the Author

Nadia Flowers is a trainer, coach, and facilitator. She is a master practitioner of neuro linguistic programming (NLP) and a certified Passion Test facilitator.

Nadia has been trained by some of the world's leading coaches and training organizations. She is on a mission to make the world a happier place. Armed with The Passion Test and her trusty coaching tool box, she helps people find their passions and live them fully. Nadia is convinced that enduring happiness & success is the result of living a life aligned with one's passions.

Nadia is hopelessly passionate about helping people live a life they love.

She lives in Wellington, New Zealand, with her husband and two young daughters, and when she's not obsessing about passion and purpose, she can be found in her fabulous kitchen baking treats for friends and family.

http://www.nadiaflowers.com

CAN YOU LOVE WHAT YOU DO AND GET WELL PAID FOR IT?

Shivani Gupta and Scott Orpin

You might be thinking: Why would you want to find your passion and purpose at your work or job?

For both of us, passion and purpose that were linked to our jobs was a foreign concept. We were guided into careers and jobs that were safe, secure, and, funnily enough, for the same company with the hope and expectation that we would be looked after. It never crossed our minds that we could work in a job that we *loved*.

This is true for most of us. Our experience in working with people in businesses, as leaders and employees over many years, is that the fifty years of work most of us do is a struggle, a compromise, and an obligation. For many people, their whole life is spent working in a job they hate, for a boss they dislike, or for a business that they do not feel connected to.

Our passion is to change this.

We believe you can find your passion and consequently have a sense of purpose, and get paid well to do it. When you really look at it, many people have discovered this and are living the life they want.

In our twenties, we started to imagine what life could be like. *Could we actually do what we love and live the life as we want?* We allowed ourselves to get caught in the trap where work was just a job. A means to an end. A way to pay the bills. All our discretionary effort went on outside work activities. We had glimpses of what we might be passionate about, but then ignored them due to fear of the unknown or fear of change. This guidance is like the streaks of sunlight shining through after the rain storm, yet we were scared to trust that the sun is *always* shining behind the clouds, as Wayne Dyer had once said.

The last fifteen years for both of us have been a long journey to unearth our passions and to refine, reshape, and create our purpose to a place where we would get paid to do what we love. One of our passions is that we love to help people change their perceptions of their work, career, and potential through discovering what they are really passionate about.

We have chosen to live a life with passion rather than spend fifty years wishing we were doing something else. Imagine if this was you. What difference would it personally mean to you, to your state of mind, to your health, to the way you would be as a partner, and to the role model you could be as a parent if you did what you truly loved? What impact could you have on your community and society if you worked in your areas of passion with a big purpose? The risk we all face is not living life to our potential. We often refer our coaching clients to the Wayne Dyer challenge: "You don't want to die with your music still inside you."

Your music can and must be heard through your work.

The impact of following a passion or pursuing a new purpose in your life is that you may have to leave the known, the comfortable, what is expected of you, and what you think you should do as your current work. It might mean you have to re-establish yourself, learn new skills, meet new people, and do new things that you have told yourself you can't do.

We are not sure we have what it takes to make the changes and we are unsure we have enough energy when the going gets tough. Instead, we often take the path of least resistance.

Our expertise is helping people love their work, either in their current role or in one we help them create. In our combined forty-year work experience, most of it spent in coaching leaders in businesses, we have found out that people are tired of working for the sake of it and are frustrated with their bosses lack of understanding of their roles and contribution. They are frustrated their employees don't treat the business like they do. They feel increasingly disconnected to the direction and vision of the organization. This has a ripple effect in other areas of their life where they begin to resent their partner or children.

Frustrations *do* still exist even when you love your work. However from our experience, when you love what you do, it is much easier for you to deal with tough moments, hard days, challenging people, and irate customers simply because you will boast the energy and desire needed to change what needs to be. Not only that, but when you are inspired, you end up inspiring your partner, family members, friends, and people in your community, let alone the people who you work with.

We have had the amazing opportunity to observe, read, and learn with global masters such as John Demartini, Jack Canfield, Loral Langmeier, and Janet Bray Attwood. We have invested heavily in our own learning because we wanted to continue shifting ourselves and creating a more passionate life. We have come to admire these masters as great examples of people that live their purpose and passion to the fullest. They cannot simply fake it for all those years. They truly believe in what they are doing.

So should everyone else.

Working with these people (and we are very grateful for the opportunity), we want to share what we have been able to create so far. Both of us have quit our corporate careers, despite high-paying positions, to have more time with our children, to have more time dedicated to our health, and to make conscious decisions of who we have to hang out with.

This journey has had its challenges including our own fears, and there were times when people have criticized us or have not returned our love. Many would see it as hard work. Sometimes we do too.

If you would like to work in your area of passion and to clarify your big *why*, then here are the tips we use with leaders and employees in organizations that may help you.

1. Identify your top five passions.

   Do The Passion Test created by Janet and Chris Attwood. This will clarify your top five passions. You need to stay true to your passions rather than those of other's.

2. Find your *why*.

   This is about identifying why you are doing what you are. We spend more time on what we do rather than why we do it. Every global master we have observed had a big *why*, even bigger than themselves. John Demartini said, "When the *why* becomes big enough, the *how's* take care of themselves." Check out a TED clip from Simon Sinek, those seventeen minutes are worth investing to be inspired.

3. Our PASSION Model.

Here are some key questions to shift your work that we ask our clients.

- **P** – Purpose

    i. When you leave your role, what would be the legacy of what you would have done?

    ii. Will anyone care?

    iii. What would you like your legacy to be?

- **A** – Associations

    i. What are your work relationships like?

    ii. Do they add to your well-being or take away from it?

    iii. What are the relationships you would like at work?

- **S** – Strength

    i. What do you think you are really good at?

    ii. What do others think you are good at?

    iii. Does your current work/career allow your strengths to come out?

- **S** – Style

    i. Do you know your own style?

    ii. How well do you understand why others act the way they do?

    iii. Does your job allow your true self to shine?

- **I** – Invest

    i. Do you consider yourself still fresh and learning in your job?

    ii. What have you done to stay ahead of others in your field?

    iii. If you continue to do what you have been doing, will you get different results (i.e. promotions, money, satisfaction) in the future?

- **O** – Options

    i. If you want to do something different, what would that be?

    ii. If you are working in your area of passion? How could you grow this further? Are you playing a big enough game?

    iii. Who is doing what you would love to do? How are they doing this different to you?

- **N** – Navigate

    i. What are your plans and actions to achieve your dreams?

    ii. Do you have a ninety-day, twelve-month, and five-year plan to shift the game to something you want?

    iii. How are you going to hold yourself accountable for the actions you make? Can an accountability coach help you?

Most of us in the West will have about four thousand weeks in our life... if we are fit and healthy. That's it. Where are you right now? One thousand? Two thousand? Three thousand maybe? How many weeks do you have left? With the time left, *now* is the right time to start living and working with your passions.

We are not suggesting you make radical changes straight away. Take your time to explore, learn, and plan before making major changes. Get some support for that journey.

If you are already doing what you love, are you getting the recognition and rewards you want? Can you do more? Are you playing a big enough game? What is the next level: your town, state, country, or the globe? There is no stopping you when you are working in your area of passion.

We have found our passion, which is to help others find theirs.

Hope you find yours too!

About the Authors

Shivani and Scott believe that their *why* is to inspire, challenge, and help transform people's lives and help people *discover* their passions.

Shivani started her career as an electrical engineer and worked in senior management corporate roles until her life-altering trip to Nepal, where she uncovered her true passion. Ten years later Shivani became CPO (chief passion officer) of the Passionate People Institute, working with global companies.

Scott has been transforming organizations for over twenty years in senior human resources corporate leadership positions. Scott is the people strategist and executive coach of the Passionate People Institute, working with global companies.

Scott and Shivani have four kids ranging between two and seventeen years of age.

http://www.passionatepeopleinstitute.com

ARE YOU IN TUNE WITH THE INFINITE?

Lydia Teodorowych

There is a Divine sequence running throughout the Universe; a sequence beyond the human ego or will, yet one that runs through it as well as beyond it. To come into harmony with this Divine sequence is to come into the higher laws and forces that shape the Universe. Once on this energetic pathway and flowing in tune with them so they can work in conjunction with us we can come into this most wondrous energetic flow and sequence which guides the soul to success.

This is the secret of all success. It is the way of coming into possession of unknown riches and the realization of undreamed of powers.

Everything that has ever been or will ever be is connected by a golden thread. What we think of as a secret is known by all before it is made manifest by the one who chooses to make it real.

This golden thread is made of a vibration of truth. It is the Universal truth that all have access to but not all choose as the rigors of modern life dictate the pace of their life into an endless cycle of work, eat, and sleep with little time for re-creation, re-gene-airation, meditation, or contemplation.

The golden thread runs through the lives and the teachings of those who have gone before us, who have shone their light for each of us to follow and learn from until we ourselves become that beacon in the stormy sea of life. The prophets, seers, saviors, sages, saints, and women and men of great and lasting power have followed their path in accordance with law.

That which one has done and created and achieved, all may do and expand upon.

This same golden thread enters into the lives of everyone on this planet called Earth. Those in this hectic world who only look at surviving and not bettering themselves or humanity after time, lose sight of this thread and exchange their power for impotence; abounding health and strength for weakness; suffering perfect peace for pain and unrest; fullness and plenty for poverty of whatever nature.

To live a life of abundance, empowerment of the self is crucial. Each one of us is building our own world. We build from within ourselves through the strength of our desires and attract the outcome from without. The building block from which we build is *thought*. Thought is a vital living force within itself being the most vital, subtle, and irresistible force there is. It is the energy of attraction and the creative power of the reality we live in.

Every form is first a thought and the intention that we put our attention on creates the energy that brings our desires to us.

Like builds like and like attracts like; that which is of the same vibration attracts its likeness.

Only when thought becomes energized does it become more subtle and far more powerful in its workings. This energizing of thought is in accordance with Universal law and is within each and everyone of us should we so choose to benefit ourselves of its energetic creative authority to use in our daily lives.

Everything is first worked out in the unseen ethers, the energetic field of all potential, the fertile canvas of the imagination and inspirational creation. From this unseen ethereal realm, the seeds of creation are born and manifest into a physical reality. That which is unseen is the cause; that which is seen is the effect.

It is this unseen realm that is the fertile ground from which all cause is born. The nature of effect is always determined and sculpted by the nature of its cause.

Whether you are an optimist or a pessimist is irrelevant. The way in which one differs from the other is that one is of positive, forward-moving vibration and the other is of static, restrictive vibration. To look at the point of view of each, they are both right as they are the creators of their own reality. This then is the pivotal point in the determination of a life… whether it is a life of power or impotence, ease or pain, success or failure.

A person with a positive attitude to life views it in its entirety and in relationship to life around them and the myriad of possibilities available to achieve a successful outcome. A person with a negative slant on life sees life from a limited one-sided, often blinkered, point of view and creates accordingly. One is illumined by wisdom; the other stands in Aristotle's cave looking at the shadows on the walls and happily living in limited ignorance.

Each one is building their world from within and the building is determined by their point of view on the same situation. One creates heaven on earth the other creates the opposite. Each one affects the world around them in the degree of the strength of the vibration they send out to the world around them and attract the like to themselves.

Life is always about that which you are prepared to create and accept, whether you accept being stopped by an issue or choose to move around it by using a different way of thinking about it.

Consider the river. It runs quickly after the rain. Where there is a rock in the middle that obstructs its way, the river goes around and continues. So it is in our lives where we can gently go with the flow of the infinite and sweep past an obstacle to continue our journey.

We all have the predominant characteristics of having a positive or negative outlook. *We* choose how we use our energy – we either waste it on unnecessary things or use it effectively in our lives – to make the most of what we have and create the most positive of futures. By our own making, hour by hour, we create our own Heaven or Hell on earth and in the degree that we are making one or the other for ourselves we help to make it for the entire world around us.

Heaven is a place or space of harmony and Hell is a word from the old English meaning to build a wall around; to separate. To be *helled* was to be shut off from. So if there is such a thing as harmony, there must be that something one can be in right relation with or in the flow of, for to be in right relation with anything is to be in harmony with it, i.e to be *one with* it. Conversely, if there is such a thing as being *helled* or shut off and separated from, there must be that something from which one is held, shut off from, or separated from. So what is it that we are *helled* from? And what are we in the flow of or in harmony with? The answer is the same for both: the creative all-potent life-giving flow... of the Universe.

What is the Single Truth That is Central in This Universe?

The single truth that permeates the whole of creation is the golden thread of the vibrational energy emanating from the creation of infinite and *unmanifested* possibilities. This thread is woven into the tapestry of this Universe and the fabric of which we are made of and vibrate with. It is the matrix of creation.

This thread animates all. It manifests itself in all and through all; it is the self-existent principle of life from which all has come and from where all is continuing to come. It is the energetic vibration of life manifest both physically and ethereally, in the seen and the unseen world. It is the energy of where we have come from, where we are now, and what we are creating in our future. The thread of the tapestry – of which is now being placed on the loom – is waiting for us to create an exquisite possibility that has not been manifested yet and is waiting to explode in unimaginable colors and unique design.

Our lives are intricately and exquisitely woven within the matrix of creation and are an integral part of it. We are no different than the essence of creation in quality although we differ in degree or depth of hue. We are one with creation and it runs through us as it does through all that is created. If we have the golden thread of creation running through us as it runs through all that is manifest, and as yet *unmanifested*, then the degree of the golden thread of creation is identical in quality with its source in the same way that a drop of water taken from its source; the ocean has the same characteristics identical with the ocean. That is: The essence is the same; the quantity is different. It is not possible to be any other way.

In other words, so far as the quality of life is concerned, we are in essence the same, yet as far as the degree or hue, we are vastly different; the microcosm is the degree or the hue of the macrocosm.

So we are one with the creation as the creation manifests within and through us as it always has and will continue to do so. The only difference being in degree; not essence.

If we can agree that this is in reality the case, then can we not follow the line of thought and creative experience that in the degree we open to this golden thread of creation the deeper the hue will be used in our lives. As we open to the unhindered flow of creative life-force washing through us and allowing us to open by degrees more and more fully to our own limitless potential, we allow the limitless matrix of creation to bloom. It is by virtue of our human-ego that we limit ourselves by not being aware of where we come from and what we are a part of.

By unleashing this awesome power from within human constraints to allow greater depth of limitlessness to enter the physical vessel that we inhabit, we gain greater understanding and knowledge of ourselves and step out of our limiting belief systems that bind us into inactivity and impotence. It is the goal of this physical experience to feel the limitations and then to step out of them into limitless abundance and a creation bursting with unique opportunity and potential.

As always, the choice is up to the degree of hue permitted into each human being, as to how much depth is chosen to flow through their life creation on this jewelled blue planet.

To disclose the great laws underlying the workings of the interior, which shape the cause of physical reality, is the aim. Simplicity and clarity are the main mode of presenting the Universal truths. These truths can then be taken and infused into everyday life so that manifesting a desired outcome can become a physical reality. No longer can the excuse of theory or speculation be used but the fact of positive knowledge and physical proof in life is the seen and measurable outcome.

About the Author

Lydia is a highly creative master manifester, ably grounding ideas into physical reality, a mother of three children, successful businesswoman, and published author living her dream on her *little piece of Heaven on Earth.*

Through her lateral thinking and seeking she has already resolved many of her health issues and has grown healthier and more youthful with age.

Lydia has an infectious sense of humor and can turn difficult situations around with workable solutions. She is deeply compassionate with the ability to have real insights into other people's issues. Her views are long-term big picture scenarios with flexibility in order to find the best way to achieve the most favorable outcome. And when she hasn't been able to resolve something tosses it to the Universe saying, "Here, You fix this now!"

She shares her wisdom with those who are ready to listen and consciously want to manifest their life.

http://www.lydiateodorowych.com

WHAT'S YOUR STORY?

David Saywell

What's the point?

What is the meaning of life? Why are we here? What's my purpose? What is my passion?

Questions: Certainly mind-opening, consciousness-expanding ones! For some, there is no right or wrong answer; for others I'm not sure I want to know the answer!

However, if you're searching for clarity, at best, these questions alone can only lead to temporary insanity!

Let's take a quick trip for a moment beyond the need to find your passion and purpose in life and *step into the realm* of pure positive energy, joy, freedom, expansion, unlimited potential, instant manifestation, and of an exciting, thrilling life.

Skills you think you have are lined up on shelves for your choosing. Answers to questions you've yet to contemplate are waiting to be delivered. You are supremely intelligent, vital, fit, and articulate, and anything else you need to be in the moment.

Now, retain what you know, what you've seen, and what you've experienced from this.

Are you in that realm?

When you are, and when you're ready, unleash your inner creative genius in this abundant place. Notice that there's no limit to what you can be, do, or have! Time and money are no obstacles. You can have anything and do anything whenever you like. If you don't know something, you can learn it. Skills you think you don't have are lined up other realm, come back to the present moment and answer...

What's your purpose? What's your passion?

I'd like you to take a second to consider these two questions and then read on:

How would you feel if you had to answer them right now? Kinda brings you back down to earth a bit, doesn't it? In one world you can be, do, or have anything you desire whenever you like, and in the other you have to choose one or two if you're lucky!

For so many years, I've been led to believe that I need to know or get clear about what my passion and purpose are in order to be truly happy in life. I'd tell myself, "I know I'm here to do something great, I just don't know what it is yet." But I'd experience so much anguish over the need to choose something and feel so constrained by the limitation of leaving so many things off of my list that I'd simply stop trying to figure it out or arrive at a conclusion that I knew wasn't right for me.

It just didn't seem fair!

I have a list as long as my arm of stuff that I enjoy doing, so how was it possible to choose one over the other? In some cases it was easy. For example, spending time with my family and having fun or going snowboarding. The thought of never being able to go snowboarding again is depressing but I'll choose my family every time if I had to choose, and that's the key.

Do I really have to choose?

Why can't I just allow myself to live life? Why can't I just allow myself to sift through the experiences, exploring and discovering new ideas and opportunities to live life more fully?

Why can't I just live a life-long journey of self-discovery; defining my passions and true calling along the way? Why can't I be comfortable in knowing that it's a never-ending process and that it's never really done, and that's why it's so exciting, interesting, and fun? Every new experience adds to the foundation and gives a new vantage point from which to identify new opportunities for new ideas and experiences.

An infinite cycle of growth, expansion, and adventure for the thrill of it... now that's something to be passionate about and something worth purposefully creating!

Please don't get me wrong. I love setting goals, taking The Passion Test, dreaming about what the future holds – which are all great ways for expanding my desires and reality – and finding new adventures and ways of *being* I had never before realized I wanted. But not for a moment can any of these things possibly define or encapsulate who I really am because who I am is constantly changing, growing, and expanding.

It's great to make lists of what you'd like to experience and stuff you'd like to have, to list ways you would like to grow; spiritually, intellectually, and emotionally, and to discover ways you'd like to contribute to society or to the world.

If you're at a point in your life where you can list three or four things that you're deeply passionate about and you know exactly what you want to do with your life perhaps you know what your calling is or your higher purpose, more power to you! You will have more clarity, intent, and focus as your journey through life continues.

Regardless of where you are, whether you have no idea of what your passion and purpose are or you're crystal clear on them, your next experience in this world is the beginning of the next of the next of the next and so on. The only thing you really have to do is live life.

This was one of the most important lessons I've learned. Whenever I've been worrying about how I'm going to do something for a project I need to finish, or stressing about what I'm going to do in the next stage of my life or trying to figure out why I'm here, I chop and change between possibilities. And when I second guess myself, questioning my ability to decide, all I'm really doing is getting bogged down, muddying the waters of my clarity, and detracting from my focus.

The times I've been able to achieve the best outcomes from situations like I've described are when I've been able to let go of the need to find the answer *right now*. I literally stop what I'm doing and quite simply do something else that makes me feel good; the first thing that pops into my mind I'll do, and then the next and the next, going with the flow, riding the waves of inspiration, being ever more decisive as I move from experience to experience throughout the day.

Being decisive creates a lineup of energy, momentum, and freedom as you move through your life. If you're indecisive, you're splitting the focus of the energy in contradictory ways. This is what holds you back and detracts you from your clarity, making you more uncertain. Moments of indecision are unpleasant and we want and need to feel good, so let's remove the need for indecision and allow the good stuff to flow in. Let's remove the angst and stress from the *all or nothing* feelings we get when contemplating our life's purpose and delight in our ability to make a choice, be fully present with it, revel in it, and make it the best choice we can possibly make by allowing it to be.

I'll never forget what happened the first time I truly let go, wiped the slate clean, and started over. I was twenty-seven at the time and had resigned from my day job as a systems analyst, gave up on desperately searching for meaning, and for the next twelve months set out on the first real adventure of my life. I didn't have any real plan for what I was going to do and was content to live day to day and see what turned up.

In that time I found my desire to be heard, discovered my gift for healing and Universal knowledge, and researched the transformation of consciousness and the fractal nature of time. I created the illustrations that are now included in my first book, started writing again for the first time in nearly ten years, helped teach well over a hundred people how to heal themselves and others, and welcomed my first baby into the world.

Toward the end of that time of discovery, I was asked to speak at an event where we were teaching energetic healing techniques. I drove about three hours to the event early in the morning and still didn't know what I was going to talk about. It was the largest group of people I'd spoken to (with the exception of our wedding) and the first time I'd had an audience who had paid to be there.

I was stressed and nervous!

I had plenty of time before the event started. So after I parked the car, and familiarized myself with the function room, I found a coffee shop around the corner and found a quiet space to sit and relax. It occurred to me that my story was the reason I was here and it'd be the easiest thing for me to remember, especially at this late stage! So basically, I was going to wing it!

When the time came, I was introduced and I took my place on stage, looked around at everyone looking at me, forced a deep breath, tried to relax and started to tell my story. It's hard to describe but it was like I went to another place and the words I was speaking were streaming through me. I was very much focused internally and not noticing the people around me, in a way, I guess I was truly speaking from the heart. What happened next... is the part I love the most.

For a brief moment I paused and looked out to the audience. The first thing I saw was my friend and colleague looking back at me with a beaming smile and a genuine heartfelt adoration in her eyes, and as I looked around so was everyone else in the room, hanging on my every word.

Looking back, it's truly a treasured memory and a profound insight into my purpose in life that I could never have imagined without having lived the experience in the first place.

So, what's the point?

We get to be here, we get to live here, and we get to experience what it's like to create *here*. We get to go to places we've never been before and meet people we've never met before. We get to *be*!

And in every moment of our being we are further defining our experience. We don't need to write our story before we start, we should be happy to start and write our story as we go.

There is nothing that you cannot be, do or have. Whatever you want... will be!

About the Author

David is an author, writer, poet and speaker with a self-described *unique take on life*. He writes and speaks on topics related to personal and spiritual development.

David has a heartfelt desire to share his experiences and work at the leading edge of creation in the New Earth, inspiring others to do the same.

Following an intense and spiritual six-month odyssey through some of the most remote parts of Australia, David now resides in a small country town north of Melbourne.

Live the full expression of your soul's desire... now! There are no limits. This is just the beginning...

http://www.davidsaywell.com

YOUR SECOND CHANCE AT FULFILLING YOUR TRUE PURPOSE

Shelby Alexander Griggs

Many of us often live for years not knowing our true purpose on this earth. We take on roles that appear to be the natural progression for us and we spend time focusing on doing that well. We secretly dream of something bigger, something more meaningful, but feel that so much time has passed and necessity has superseded our pipe dreams. I'm here to tell you that every day God gives you breath and that there is still time.

I remember the day I woke up and realized I hated my job. I no longer felt relevant and certainly didn't think I was making a difference. I got tired of motivating people to come to work and inspiring them to reach higher. I became extremely frustrated when I would have a one-on-one meeting with my employees and talk about their next-level goals and they often responded with irritation as though I was intruding.

I desired to work with people who wanted to think, be, and do better in their lives. Once I knew what my purpose was on this earth, nothing could keep me from walking towards it. Please understand, this did not happen overnight. You have to seriously assess your goals and meditate on it. I talked to so many people but never got my answers until I stopped talking and started praying. What I know for sure is that you will never truly be in your *element* until you're in a space where what you do is as easy as breathing.

During the time I was searching for my purpose, I often thought about what I dreamed of being when I was a little girl. I reflected on what people told me over the years about what my character entailed. I actually sat down with my parents and other family members to discuss my childhood and the type of person they recalled me being. You will be surprised as to what you discover when you explore your past.

I remember when I got my first corporate-job promotion. It was the most exciting and proudest moment of my life. I worked so hard at an entry level position to finally be recognized for my skills and leadership ability. Soon, I began to gain the attention of senior leadership on the executive floor. Each would call me into their office to tell me how they saw something special in me and wanted to take me under their wing. Most were blowing smoke but there were a few who were sincere about helping me take my career to the next level.

A senior executive in particular did just that and I would say that he shaped my career and taught me some valuable life lessons.

He was from New York and had moved to the Deep South to take over my division. He seemed a bit out of place with what was said, his Yankee accent, and cranky disposition. He was smart and tough at the same time. He reminded me so much of my dad and I later discovered that he was a Vietnam War veteran just like my father.

I thought he would be the perfect mentor for me.

With his guidance and support, I successfully climbed the corporate ladder and felt that I was truly in my zone.

For years, I was confident that being a corporate manager was my calling until I turned thirty. All of a sudden, I was feeling like there had to be more out there for me. Despite my success, I wasn't fulfilled in my life. I didn't think I was making a difference and I began to pray and meditate about what God's purpose was for me. Every single day, I was asking Him to reveal what it was that I was supposed to do on this earth.

Whenever I had conversations with friends and family about it, they thought I was crazy for wanting to leave such a successful career. I often had my employees in my office requesting to meet with me to discuss their career plans. The conversations always transitioned into their life plans. The word started to spread and I began to have other employees in the office requesting the same from me.

One day, someone walked up to me and said, "Shelby, the advice you gave me really helped. I want you to know that you changed my life."

I shrugged my shoulders and refused to take credit but soon more people were telling me those exact words.

A few years later, I had an opportunity to see Oprah Winfrey in person. I attended an event they have every ten years in her hometown to celebrate her showcase on how far the town had progressed. I was so excited to finally see her in person because it was almost impossible to get tickets to her television show without going on a waiting list for years.

It was a small town in Mississippi and they were a very intimate group with lots of opportunity to interact with her. As I sat there listening to her speak, I took notice of the audience. Women and men were on the edge of their seats hanging on her every word. She was very casual with her presentation and seemed extremely comfortable addressing the crowd.

At that very moment, I got it. She had a gift. She had God-given talents with the ability to connect with people; connect with their hearts. Here's the difference between Oprah and the rest of the people still searching for a purpose: she knows her gifts and she's using them. She's not going against the grain but flowing with the Universe. I have learned that when it gets really tough trying to make something happen, chances are it's not the right thing to do. The will of God's purpose for you on this earth isn't hard or difficult. I heard Oprah say once that even though it was her ultimate dream to be a newscaster, it was never easy. It wasn't until she got demoted to a local morning show that she felt like it was easy as breathing.

When I presented at my very first seminar, I felt the exact same feeling. At first, I was anxious and nervous but once I got up there, it was like breathing. I finally stood in my own light. I was comfortable and allowed God to guide me through it all. It was life-changing for me and I was never the same again. After that epiphany, everything I did, every path I took, I carried that sense of purpose with me.

So… you may be someone who had a dream to do something but life got in the way and you took the necessary route. You may feel discouraged because although you love your spouse and wouldn't change having your children for the world, there is still a longing for that dream. You know that dream? The one you are afraid to say out loud in fear that your family and friends think you're silly for having?

Know that it's not too late.

The journey to your true purpose may have been delayed but it will never be denied. When I worked in the corporate world, people often asked what I was doing working there. They saw my gift and were puzzled as to why I was wasting my time on them. I would always reply, "This is just my layover until I get to my final destination."

So, how do you get to the beginning of at least mapping out your journey to purpose? I want to share with you what I believe are the essential steps.

5 Steps to Fulfilling Your True Purpose

1. **Acknowledge Your Past**: Talk to family and childhood friends about your personality growing up. I always suggest this because it's easy to forget the impressionable kid you used to be before life took over. As a kid, you wanted to be President of the United States and really believed it was possible. This exercise will surely get your creative juices flowing and remind you of what you dreamed to be when life was simple.

2. **Write Out a Plan**: Start journaling your ideas, dreams, or goals. In the beginning, I had a really cute and decorative journal that I quickly outgrew! I then had spiral notebooks everywhere with goals and my big dreams in them. I also attached realistic dates to them. Just writing down your dreams isn't going to be enough; you have to put action to it eventually.

3. **Find a Mentor**: This was the best investment I could have ever made in myself. What you have to remember is that *your* dream is just that: yours. Your family and friends who are not achieving at the level you aspire to be won't be much motivation. Plus, it would be challenging for you to learn and progress in your goals consulting people who don't understand your plight. If not a mentor, find a mastermind group to bounce ideas off of.

4. **Seek a Higher Power for Direction and Course Correction**: For me, prayer is a priority. I cannot make a decision, go on stage to speak, or even contribute this chapter without connecting spiritually to my higher power which is God. However you pray it's important to stay spiritually connected to your purpose along this journey. It will not be easy, especially if you have established in your mind that what you're doing now is the end all be all. This will most definitely require a shift in your mindset if you're ever going to see your dream come to fruition.

5. **Do Your Research**: There is a scripture in the Holy Bible that says, "Faith without works is dead." You must do the work if you're ever going to be doing something different in your life. Do your research no matter what it is. If you want to write a book, research writers' groups in your area. Follow other authors on social media to see how they're doing it. The internet can be a bit overwhelming but there are some extremely useful sites out there if you drill your searches down. The best thing you can do at the very beginning is find someone who is successfully doing what you dream to do. Sign up for their newsletters so that you get a feel of how they communicate to their followers.

Please let me make one thing perfectly clear: your purpose is *your* purpose. It's not anyone else's. Whatever it is, stay true to your own voice and do not deviate from that. Once you find the courage to start speaking about your dreams, people will try to deter you or redefine them. Stay the course. Consult your mentor or a group of like-minded people. Trust me when I say that authenticity is critical when you're talking about pursuing your true purpose. Remember that it's not too late to fulfill your passion and purpose on this earth. You are just at your layover place until you reach your final destination. As long as you have breath in your body, all things are possible!

I'm excited for you and all of the possibilities you have before you. I would love to connect with you so that I can stay abreast of your successes. It's time to live your life with purpose!

About the Author

Since 1998, Shelby Alexander Griggs has inspired women with countless empowerment seminars and one on one coaching sessions. She is the author of *Opening the Door to Your True Purpose*, and contributing author of *Adventures in Manifesting: Health and Happiness*. Shelby is also a radio show host for Girl Talk with Shelby on ArtistFirst Radio Network. She has been featured in Dallas Child Magazine and held a board member seat for the Dallas Network of Career Women in Dallas, Texas.

http://www.shelbyalexandergriggs.com

THE MOST IMPORTANT VALUE
YOU CAN GIVE

Bob Doyle

If we want to receive abundance in our lives – and that can be in the form of money, relationships, or just *stuff* – we have to provide some kind of energetic value to the Universe. We do that by fully contributing what we have to give; by being who we truly are; by following our passions and our sense of purpose.

What we do during the bulk of the day and how we feel about it plays a large part in our vibrational state. Most people tend to set aside only a small part of their day to intentionally put their emotional focus on the life they want to create through some kind of visualization exercise, meditation, or some other *technique*. Remember, the hour or so per day that we may spend doing some kind of visualization exercise is only a small portion of our waking life. If we don't do something to shift this energetic balance, it will be the thoughts and feelings that we're having when we're *not* visualizing that dictate what comes into our lives.

It stands to reason, then, that if you are working at a job that is unsatisfying, or if you are otherwise unhappy with the occupation that takes up eight-plus hours of your day, that is a lot of time to be energetically vibrating at a frequency you do not want the Universe to match.

If your inspired vision gets checked at the door of your workplace, then you are really sending the Universe mixed signals about what you perceive the reality of your life to be.

Let's assume that you wake up in the morning and spend time envisioning your perfect life. You get into the feeling and shift your vibration in a way that will accelerate the fulfillment of those desires. Then you think, "Okay, back to the real world. Gotta go to work." For the next ten hours, your thoughts are mired in a wholly unsatisfying pattern of thought that simply works to attract more of the same.

How much of your true value are you really contributing when so little of the *real you* is in your work? Not much! The amount of value that comes back to you in the form of a true feeling of abundance, joy, and prosperity will most likely not be as much as you'd hoped, despite the hours of labor you are putting in.

The hours are not the value. Value is not gauged by how hard you work. Value comes from answering this question: What is your contribution to the Universe? This is a more accurate assessment of value, because the quality of your contribution, or your energy, will improve as you live the life you truly desire to live, instead of the one you have been living by default without any real choice based in passion.

Perhaps you're thinking, "I have to go to work, though! Until this *attraction stuff* starts working for me, I have to pay the bills somehow! I can't wait around for the Universe to deliver. I need money now!"

It is just so easy to get caught up in this kind of thinking. It seems logical. After all, there are bills that are due, and your bank account might not have the money to cover them.

What perpetuates your situation is the emotion associated with the statement, "I have got to pay my bills!" Here's the harsh reality: The Universe isn't looking out for your best interests. That's your job. The Universe delivers precisely in alignment with your vibration, whether it's a vibration you're putting out consciously or not.

So what is the obvious fix to this *job* thing? Well, it is simple. Find out what you love to do, and do that. The obvious objection comes, "I'd love to, but it will not pay the bills," which makes that defensive excuse completely true for whoever says it. There is generally a lot of emotion around a statement like that, and it vibrates *lack* like crazy.

I know this from personal experience.

But here is what was true for me. When I first was out there trying to make a living at what I loved to do, it immediately became a job. Something felt at stake. There was a *do or die* thing about it. Some of the passion and joy of the activities (and I tried several) was sucked right out, because I suddenly needed to make money with it.

What is the effect on your vibration when you engage in this kind of thinking? It plummets. You are now vibrating with stress, fear, and worry.

In your previous attempts to live your dream, you might have had fun... but were you also aware of the Law of Attraction? Did you have a clear vision of the life you truly wanted to design? Or were you going through your day-to-day life, doing what you loved but with no clear direction or with a nagging feeling in the back of your mind that your life might not pan out exactly as you'd hoped?

Consider this really carefully. The answer to *why your attempt at making a living from your passions did not work in the past* lies in the honest answers to these questions. If you had no clear vision, then raising your vibrations by doing what you loved only served to bring you more of whatever it is you were vibrating or thinking about. If you were not creating a future vision, then your thoughts were probably just on your day-to-day activities, so you remained where you were. When you did not see *progress*, it is because you really did not define (and generate positive emotion around) what progress actually was or how it could be measured. As a result, you may have started to second-guess your decision to do what you loved for a living.

The moment that happened, you began your descent. Because you were not consciously aware that you should have reversed that thinking immediately, you just followed this counter-productive thought process downward, which resulted in the manifestation of negative situations.

Then you made the conclusion, "Well, I tried it and I failed." And you started looking for a new *real job* when that was not necessarily your only option, and certainly not the way to attract wealth, particularly if you simply settled for a job that did not fulfill you.

All of this underlines the theme of this book, which is to be who you truly are. Do what you are meant to do without worry or apology. As a result, your vibration will naturally rise and your predominant thoughts, desires, and intentions will come to you more readily. Why? Because when you are being fully and completely who you truly are, contributing your natural, unique gifts to the world and loving virtually every moment of your life, you will put out vibrations in precise alignment with what you want to experience in your life, and in the process you will contribute maximum value to the Universe as a whole! The reward for that is your ability to live whatever life you want.

Pretty nice reward, I'd say.

About the Author

Bob Doyle is the CEO of Boundless Living, Inc., and author of the #1 best-selling book *Follow Your Passion - Find Your Power*. Since 2002, Bob has been teaching principles of living life by design utilizing the principles of the Law of Attraction.

His Wealth Beyond Reason program has long been recognized as one of the most complete and usable online curriculums in the Law of Attraction, and gained the attention of the producers of the film and book, *The Secret*, in which Bob was one of the featured teachers.

Bob is a champion for creative self-expression and his work focuses on reconnecting people to their sense of passion and purpose and helping them to create a vision that inspires them into massive action working in concert with the natural laws of physics to realize a life of true abundance and joy!

Bob is a veteran broadcaster, music composer, author, photographer, and ukulele fanatic among other things, and encourages people to fully explore any, and all, of their passions, playing full out all the time, thus allowing the Law of Attraction to work effortlessly to attract all that they desire into their lives.

http://www.boundlessliving.com

FROM INSPIRATION... TO MANIFESTATION

Solah Nightstar

I came into this world with a remembrance. We all do.

Unless our remembrance is fostered by our culture, deep inner knowing usually becomes buried. Sometimes a major life-event such as a near-death experience rumbles our foundation, forcing us deep into the rediscovery of what we once knew. Other times we work to retain our connection, listening carefully and allowing it to guide us.

My inner knowing says, "Question everything, trust your feelings and above all else... while respecting others, do what makes you happy."

This is the story of listening to that deep inner knowing and its resulting adventures in manifesting...

Born in 1974 in suburban North America, I was fortunate to be deeply loved by parents who worked hard to ensure I had a solid upbringing. Despite these foundations, I was haunted with a longing for more; feeling a distinct disconnect between the knowledge I brought to this life and the culture I was being raised within.

I spent much time in quiet contemplation about the way the Universe works. With a head full of theories about how we might manifest our reality, it wasn't until my mid-teenage years that these ideas began revealing themselves as my truths.

At sixteen years old, and between jobs, a family member set me up with a union position in a drugstore. Learning the work of each department was enjoyable, but the location and lack of freedom to take days off when my friends were going camping challenged my free-spirited nature. The polyester striped uniform and metal bars on the doors only deepened my feelings of imprisonment.

My greatest fear in those days was to die in my uniform.

After a few years behind these bars, my work schedule harmonized with my friends' spur-of-the-moment adventures, allowing me to join them on a camping trip to an island surf town. Moments after our arrival, I made a new friend. I remember vividly the intense sense of freedom I felt there while dancing barefoot in the sand. Together, gazing out upon the ocean and speaking from my heart, I explained how my job had been preventing me from joining my friends on these excursions.

It was then that my new friend shared with me a powerful truth. "You can do anything you want in the world. You have the power to create a life you love," this messenger said.

No one had *ever* told me this before. Immediately, I felt the resonance of truth.

From that moment on my world opened up. Books began jumping off the shelf. Literally. One of the first being *The Nature of Personal Reality*, channelled by Jane Roberts. This book confirmed every idea I had pondered, while growing up, about the way our reality is constructed.

Again, deep reverberations of truth. It was time to become the conscious creator of my own life.

First, I decided to discover my ideal career. By creating a list of all the things I loved and wanted more of in my life, as well as the things I didn't, I found the vocation that felt like a perfect fit. Deciding to become a special effects makeup artist for film and television, I wanted to create kooky looking characters for inspirational children's programming.

Informed that years of volunteering and dedication were required after the schooling, I enrolled. Despite my lack of exceptional talent in this field and warnings that less than 1% of makeup artists are successful in this industry, I envisioned myself being nominated for an award. I didn't feel special talent was necessary, for I possessed vision and determination instead.

To pay the bills I took work as a bartender in a funky atmosphere surrounded by creative people my age. I worked when I wanted to and that gave me time to volunteer for makeup gigs. Knowing my dream career would be all consuming time-wise and believing in living life without any regrets, I also took a couple years off to travel and snowboard.

For ten years I was fully determined on my path and fully loving life.

Then it happened.

I felt my values shift. Although I loved my career path and was beginning to get paid gigs, I started to realize that elements of this work no longer fit who I was becoming as an adult; sixteen-hour work days fuelled by white sugar and coffee, applying chemicals to human skin in all too often unhealthy atmospheres, and taking on ethically conflicting projects simply because that's where the money was.

Would I really be happy dedicating my life to this? Was that what I really wanted?

I briefly thought that instead of entirely changing my career path, perhaps I would use what I had learned to change the industry. So I began designing my own line of animal-friendly professional makeup and tools for industry artists, which gave profits back to the causes affected by the use of traditional products.

Not far into this development (thanks to my spirit guides), an old friend showed up and was guided to share with me a big business idea he had. His idea got me so inspired that I jumped on the opportunity to collaborate. The following day I surprisingly resolved to leave my beloved beach apartment and move up to Whistler, Canada, to work with my friend. As one plan led to another in Whistler, I was taught a whole lot about business. Aside from the entrepreneurial adventures, finding my soul mate was the biggest gift I received from this three-year detour to the mountains. Announcing to the Universe that I was ready to be in a committed relationship, I knew exactly what I wanted in a partner… and that's precisely what I got!

His name is Erin. My passion for the sound of African drums led me straight to him. Attending a community drum-circle in Vancouver had been a favorite hobby and Whistler lacked this type of gathering. So the day after moving there, a friend and I decided to facilitate one. We rented space and created posters and fliers.

The first person I handed a flier to turned out to be my soul mate.

Erin and I lived together for a year at the lake in the mountains. I was working on a business plan that helped non-profits fund-raise using environmentally friendly products. I was also babysitting, doing bridal makeup, and running a little dreadlock hairstyling business on the side.

Life was blissful!

Then came the test. Was I fully ready to embrace stepping off of the path I had been dedicated to with my makeup career? Suddenly I was being presented a Special Effects Makeup Award for an indie film I had worked on two years ago. It was an open door's invitation to a successful career launch: red carpet; golden trophy; all out of the blue.

Shortly after the awards ceremony arrived test number two.

The film union called with a job invitation for a big movie. This moment was ten years in the making. But, was I ready to return to Vancouver and start work the following day?

With newly aligned values came a new answer: *no thank you.*

Soon after the clarity of being done with the makeup chapter, Erin and I were feeling the need for a larger creative living space and some city action. So back to Vancouver, and into a rare live-and-work resource building for artists, we moved.

Another dream of ten years come true!

During the transition we journeyed to Burning Man funded by an Artist in Residency program we facilitated, paying us the exact amount we had calculated needing for our trip to the desert festival.

The desert showed us more about the strength of our partnership and moving to the ARC (Artist Resource Centre) provided a fresh space to discover what my new career was to be. For the second time in my life I would reassess my skills, values, and passions to find my ideal work, this time equipped with more life experience and a better sense of who I was in relation to the world around me.

Inspiration, magic, creativity, fun, and freedom remained highly important.

Additionally, I had gained a love for small business and the power of social entrepreneurs to create positive change. I noticed how my ways had inspired others, and saw many people unaware of how much power they possessed in creating a life they loved. I then realized that the most fulfilling work for me would be to give others what I had been giving to myself: to help them manifest their *hearts' callings* and to feel the joy of walking the path illuminated by the heart.

In order to facilitate this work, I enrolled in schooling to further study metaphysics and to become a life coach.

Taking advantage of the amazing artist's building we were in, I also expanded my beloved dreadlock business and began creating fabric art, sculpting, and learning to use the kiln.

Around the same time, overwhelmed by how many worldly causes requested support, I decided that for one year I would focus on one cause, and announced it to the Universe: water. Not knowing what shape this support would take, I simply left it at that.

While in school, bartending remained a fun supplemental income. However, choosing to utilize and expand upon what I had learned about business, I wanted to find a position as an executive assistant. Due to my lack of direct experience in this position, evident on my resume, I created a unique campaign highlighting my skills and passions. More traditionally, and thinking it would be the last place I'd be discovered, I posted my resume on Craigslist. It was there that the owner of a company that restores water back to its natural, healthy state made the connection, and I became his assistant.

After about a year of this work my heart was clearly telling me that I was meant to be an entrepreneur, *not an employee*. I resolved to be done with this job and to have my dreadlock business fully sustaining me by that September.

This resolution was followed by an emailed quote request for dreadlock extensions: a new service I was offering. Promising myself I would not undercharge, I sent off the big quote.

The phone rang.

It was the artistic director for a huge circus show in Vegas. He didn't want one set of extensions; he needed thousands, and the project wouldn't start until September. In order to fulfill this order, I'd have to quit my desk-job to hire and train ten people.

Done and done.

As soon as the big circus gig wrapped up, my first solo art show took place. Over twenty-five hundred people attended my sacred studio space created to highlight the circus project, our line of inspirational stickers birthed from the trip to the desert, and my sculpting. There was also an art installation where visitors walked a life path inspiring them to take action on their own dreams.

Following this show, it was time for my amazing partner to realize *his* dream of throwing an off-grid music festival. Feeling ready to live more connected with nature for the summer we decided to purchase a mobile home to live and work from. The first day of looking for this vehicle, a super, funky converted ice-cream truck named The Dream Machine found us.

Dreamy indeed!

Adventures unending, my story continues, leaving no dreams unfulfilled. By following my heart and cultivating the connection to my knowingness, I bring my dreams *from inspiration... to manifestation.*

By investing in myself I'm now able to serve others from the truth of my core. My grand adventures in manifesting... now intertwined with yours.

Dancing in the sand, I share with you so that we can all create lives we love.

About the Author

Solah Nightstar B.Div. is a manifestation mentor, empowerment coach, Passion Test facilitator and speaker.

She works to help change-makers discover exactly what they want and to support them in creating their desired reality. She converts their inspiration... to manifestation.

Ultimately, Solah believes that by listening to our hearts and honoring our own needs, we establish greater internal balance and strength. This re-alignment with our true selves naturally radiates outwards and, from microcosm to macrocosm, we will see many of the world's biggest imbalances also begin to realign into health and harmony.

More inspiration and keys to manifestation can be found through Solah's blog and newsletter at her website.

http://www.positivelypurposeful.com

FINDING YOU THROUGH UNEXPECTED CHALLENGE

Kent Sayler

The sensation of being painfully shocked by the electricity surging through my entire body was bad enough, but it was the intensity of the very deep, loud, and crystal-clear message pounding in my head that really shocked the hell out of me. The whole experience probably only lasted for five seconds, but the memory of what had just happened to me remains vivid to this day.

This all occurred about six years ago, while my world was falling apart. After decades where life treated me quite well, I started getting clobbered by wave upon wave of unnerving surprises.

I got laid off, which at the age of forty-five had never happened to me before. That alone sent me reeling. My unemployment lasted about six months. I finally found another job. It wasn't as good as the one I originally held, but, still, it was a job and I was grateful. It was in the telecomm industry in 2003, just prior to when the industry imploded. After being there for only five months, I was out of work again!

Then, the financial problems began.

My unemployment periods had definitely created a hardship. For the very first time, I was afraid that I might not be able to care for my family. That was really scary…

Things only continued to get worse. This next wave almost killed me: my wife of twenty-two years told me she wanted a divorce. We had a great and happy marriage, but the recent turmoil in my life had become very difficult for her to take. She told me she couldn't handle the rollercoaster we were riding in our life. She felt that I let her down. I tried to fix some problems, and my solutions only made things worse. She had enough and wanted out of the marriage.

I was completely devastated by this revelation. I felt like everything I cared about – the life I had known for all those years – was being completely destroyed. There was no purpose to my life.

At one point during this dark period, when my wife and I were separated, I was praying desperately for my marriage to be saved. I remember distinctly one evening, where I was literally rocking back and forth on my bed praying so hard. Then – and I will remember this forever – I was hit by a sudden electric-shock-like sensation surging through my entire body.

I heard a loud voice telling me with utmost clarity that resolution of my marriage was *not* in the plan, and that instead, I was to be entrusted with a mission to lead a very important effort.

I started sobbing, because I had never received such a clear message from Spirit before! Of course, this was *not* the message that I wanted to hear. It was the opposite of what I was praying for! In addition, what was up with this *leading a very important effort* statement? I had no idea what this meant.

Fast forward five years…

Through a clearer perspective that was gained through time and healing, I had a new outlook on purpose. What I now know to be true is that these horribly painful moments in our lives are brought forward from a place where we think we will never recover. To our surprise, this is actually what enables a new beginning to unfold in our lives to ultimately lead us to a new destiny; a new purpose. In other words, these events that we refer to as *the worst things* to happen to us, often become the best things that ever happen to us. It just may not feel that way in the present moment that the event is occurring.

It was only at the end of my dark tunnel, after all of this completely unexpected pain and aching loss, that I woke up and discovered *me*! That horrible, scary period in my life created the opportunity for me to figure out *who I am* and what my purpose is!

These incidents in my life finally facilitated an amazing feeling of empowerment and fulfillment. For the first time, I felt that I was living a life aligned with my passions and my purpose. My personal destiny was beginning to unfold.

Through my life journey, I became aware that my passion was to help others realize their passions and align with their own life purpose. To that end, Janet Bray and Chris Attwood's Passion Test found me, and I was super-excited to become a Passion Test facilitator in 2010.

Since aligning with my own passions, I am amazed at how exciting my life has become. I am amazed at what I am manifesting. Not only do I love what I do, but I get to meet and work with some of the most positive transformational people in the world. Through all of this, I have learned to be open to whatever shows up for me as blessings from God, the Universe, and Source.

I have come to understand that such blessings rarely show up in the manner *I* think they should, but that's okay. Once I was open to letting go and living in the present, what manifested itself in my life would ultimately be way better than what I originally had planned in my mind. I love that!

In my own journey, and as I shared The Passion Test with others, it became obvious to me that each one of us needs to figure out who we are and truly be who we are! I woke up to the fact that when I am feeling the happiest and most fulfilled, I am living a passionate life of showing others how to live passionately.

I've also come to the understanding that our passions are the breadcrumbs that lead us to our destiny; our true unique purpose in life. This usually happens one step at a time, without us ever realizing what's happening.

There is something inside you that is highly powerful – your true will. When you align with the things you love, you unleash your true will and tap into your higher self, your faith, and your destiny. Discovering what makes your heart sing is the first essential step to finding true happiness, confidence, love, and a renewed success that we all deserve.

As I immersed myself in providing my unique benefits to the world, the continuation of my journey provided another key realization: *We as human beings also need to know that we are part of something bigger than ourselves – something that matters deeply to us and that we know to be really important.* It is only when we comprehend this fact that our own personal mission can begin to reveal itself to us.

Let me explain.

Life started changing in an amazing way for me after I got very clear on living through my passions, and when I started to listen and follow my intuition. Some insightful direction from my amazing experience with God resulted in my unexpected flying to Maui, Hawaii, in November to attend Vishen Lakhiani's Awesomeness Fest, where I received a very surprising awakening at the perfect time.

On the third day, we attended a presentation called Awakening the Dreamer. The name sounded vaguely familiar, but I had no idea from where. As the presentation started, I developed prickles at the back of my neck in a weird déjà vu sensation. I knew I had experienced this before… but what *was* this?

Shortly, it all became clear. This was a presentation put on through an organization called the Pachamama Alliance, titled Awakening the Dreamer, Changing the Dream. I had actually been through this symposium a year and a half before. When I attended that session back then it moved me, but there were enough distractions in my life that it did not result in any call to action on my part.

You know, the Universe does have its ways of making sure that we get the messages that we're intended to get. This time, at the Awesomeness Fest in Hawaii that God prompted me to attend, the symposium *really impacted* me.

Before we go any further, let me explain what Pachamama means. Pachamama is a word in the Quechua [Kee-chwa] language of the Andes that some translate as *Mother Earth,* but more accurately includes the sacred presence of *the Earth, the sky, the Universe, and all time.*

The highly-interactive Awakening the Dreamer symposium brings together respected scientific expertise and indigenous wisdom. It takes you gently, *yet directly,* front and center with the facts of how we in the Western World are living an unsustainable lifestyle in so many ways. It also provides poignant facts and perspectives regarding how our lifestyle choices are negatively impacting the entire planet. This experience is moving, inspiring, and empowering, as it calls participants to explore the most urgent challenges *and possibilities* for our time.

Symposiums are now being held all over the world, inspiring thousands of people to realize their tremendous potential as agents of change. They are equipping listeners to take on the challenges and opportunities of this moment in history, make positive impacts in their communities, and live a fulfilling life full of purpose.

I signed up to become a facilitator for the Awakening the Dreamer symposium, and I knew I was called to take one of the Pachamama-sponsored journeys into the Amazon to experience this for myself.

At the end of that day's powerful events, I was on sensory overload, yet exhilarated beyond words. I walked the beautiful Wailea beach that evening, where out of the blue I received the realization that I am now actually living out the subtitle of my book, *An Operator's Manual for Fulfilling Your Destiny and Making a Difference in the World*.

It really hit me for the first time that these were no longer just words that I wrote years ago, which I just happened to come to believe in. I now had received the download to the pathway to actually *live the book that I wrote*, about what had been only *ideas* for me just three years earlier!

I was so moved by this realization that back on the lanai (balcony) of my hotel room, overlooking the beautiful Hawaiian Pacific under the light of the moon, I broke down. Huge sobs of unbelievable gratitude.

I knew my next step on my journey and I knew it involved the Pachamama Alliance. My intuition guided me on this trip to ignite a new passion that was awaiting me. I didn't know anything more, and that was okay.

We never get the full picture of what we are to do – we only receive clarity when we align ourselves with our passions. Then we receive another step, courtesy of our intuition. Our job is to move forward in faith and take each step, not knowing where it will specifically lead us, or what is to come after it.

My message here is that *you have to be who you are.* Live the life that you were intended to live. To do that, whenever you are faced with a choice, a decision, or an opportunity, choose in favor of your passions and follow your intuition.

We all really do have a purpose in our lives; something that we come to know we're supposed to do at the proper time. This is something that can even provide endless benefits to others, while making our hearts sing.

Although God might give you a very loud directive in your head one day, the rest of the details happen by *listening* to the quiet, gentle voice of your intuition. It will guide you to those people, places, and things that will make your heart sing and manifest your desires. You will come to realize that you have found something truly meaningful that becomes an important part of your life and mission.

I *still* don't know exactly what Spirit meant with the proclamation that I was to be leading a very important effort. But I know deep in my heart that by doing these things I've shared with you, and by following my intuitional guidance, I am definitely moving in the direction of my ultimate assignment: my life purpose. I feel it. I know it's true, because it feels right and makes me feel so alive.

Here's to you finding and living *your* purpose with passion!

About the Author

Kent Sayler is a Live-Your-Calling coach, speaker, author, and certified Passion Test facilitator. After a successful thirty-year career in Fortune 500 and emerging technology companies and with a happy family life, Kent faced a period of devastation six years ago. This was led by a relentless combination of employment, financial, and relationship failures.

Through application of potent knowledge gained during years of a focused recovery effort, Kent has found his way out of the abyss and into a deep, genuine place of empowered renewal. He now specializes in assisting people, whose lives have gone off-course, transform their setbacks, self-doubt, and unfulfilled dreams into confidence, purpose, and a new sense of success.

http://www.findyourmissingpeace.com

ON THE POWER OF UN-WORTHINESS

Fatima Bacot

"You cannot contain those that cannot be contained."
~Abraham Hicks~

Since I was nine, thoughts filled my mind such as: *Why am I here? Was I put on this earth for a reason? What is the purpose of life?*

Later, as a teenager, concepts of revolution, anarchy, freedom, and transformation rolled through, as I embarked upon what would become a voracious search for answers, and for freedom. I felt that I was bursting to express *something* that was *truthful* about life and that my purpose involved helping others, but I just didn't know how or in what manner.

I had only the intensity of a *knowing*.

If anything has been the lynchpin to passionately living this knowing, it centers wholly upon the theme of worthiness, for simultaneously with the above, I felt cripplingly unworthy and *less than* from a very young age. I believed I was *inherently bad* and that I must have done terrible things once upon a time. I believed I was going to be neither free nor happy, nor that my life would have meaning until I had *righted all these wrongs*, and further, that if I stepped out of line (even if I didn't know quite what that line was), I would most certainly be punished.

Although it would take me decades to fully articulate, I gradually came to the realization that *imagined unworthiness* was a tyranny. The freedom to passionately live my purpose would eventually demand the complete and radical deconstruction of all belief structures founded upon *unworthiness*, and the replacement, instead, with those founded upon *freedom and wellbeing* as the intrinsic basis of the Universe.

During innumerable stages of my life, I felt cursed: cursed to know and see a heartfelt purpose and living it passionately to the fullest; cursed because no matter how hard I tried, I just couldn't get to where I wanted to be and what I had seen. Despite profound knowledge of what it felt like to live it, my experiences involved landing face-down in the mud of seeming failures because, in spite of continual and courageous leaps into the unknown, thinking *this must be it*, my feelings of exhilaration would not last. And like a voracious monster from the depths, the inner tyranny would always return, and happiness, vision, and identity would collapse.

For a very long time, I woke up depressed every morning with the agonizing thought, "I am still here." Countless times I went to sleep, pleading to die in the night for I viewed being alive not as a gift, but as a punishment, meted out for reasons vague.

I did not know then that it was my beliefs about myself and about life that led to such tyranny. I did not understand then the power of thought. I did not know then that I even had *the right* to freedom. Such was the overpowering and ingrained level of imagined worthlessness that lived like a deadly virus within.

However, equipped with such a purpose, I was not one who could be contained (and neither are you or you wouldn't be reading this). And so, in the early stages, I lived a titanic inner struggle between knowing there must be more, wanting to not be here, moving through the toxic morass of my beliefs and emotions, and feeling crazy, like I might one day stray into madness if I wasn't careful. (As any mythology or fairytale will attest, the quest is populated by all things friendly and unfriendly, and sometimes these are interchangeable.)

In my journey, and perhaps with yours, the most critical keys in crossing the bridge from unworthiness to worthiness were my overwhelming desire to be free and the persistence to continue.

I read voraciously the world's philosophers, writers, esotericists, poets, occultists, cosmologists, and mystics, looking for answers and underlining paragraph after paragraph in their books. I wanted to be free in the way I felt that great mystics and philosophers were, and that musicians and artists conveyed.

I would do anything to free myself of constraint, in the hope of making that definitive move that would finally make everything all right.

I reasoned that I would have sex because I would go to Hell for even thinking about it, so I might as well go there for actually doing it. I became a punk rocker and played bass and sang in a band for a bit because the lyrics and the songs made me feel free. I quit my job, landed in Spain and England, and looked for freedom and limitlessness on dance-floors. I sold everything I owned and bought a one-way ticket from Canada to Australia, looking for the promised land. I went to India with a copy of *A Course in Miracles*, to sit with a guru who opened me to eastern mysticism. I quit another job to study journalism to *tell the truth*, or another to start facilitating astrological readings and rebirthing sessions. I threw myself into New Age spirituality to *fix myself* as part of the shift in consciousness. I walked with a mentor that helped keep me here and to order my emotions and open me to new gifts and dimensions of myself. I suddenly started mentoring others without having a mentoring package and needing to materialize one over a weekend. I decided I wanted to bring my spiritual work to the United States, and whipped up events out of thin air. I decided to suddenly write a book and to start painting because an inner voice told me so. I married my present husband just after a few months because *it might just turn out all OK*. I moved twenty-three times in twenty-five years.

My questing (however haphazard it must appear) has all been to do with burning all inner constraints to the ground, and neither crippling fear nor being broke nor starting something I knew nothing about would stop me.

An invisible barrier, however, remained. Yes, I possessed much inner strength and had forged many gifts for which I was immensely grateful, but I was exhausted from all the looking and not finding. It was at this point that I came face to face with that nefarious and shape-shifting lynchpin called *unworthiness*. Its cunning toxicity generated a dangerous Universe. It was then that I sought to burn down to the ground that lynchpin... and see what lay beyond it.

I discovered that humanity's diverse interpretations of life (good and evil), purpose, and the infinite, differed from age to age, from civilization to civilization, and even from one present-day culture to another. Tracing a theme such as unworthiness took me to interpretations that originated in times when understandings of the Universe were more limited than they are now. I decided that what applied not two thousand, but only two years ago, perhaps no longer applied. And if it did, according to whom, and why did I render them true? I wondered what actually made these interpretations true, except for a belief in them. I came to understand that, for millennia, human beings have asked the same perennial questions that I asked when I was nine, but that the answers were always changing.

Always.

So, I wondered what would happen if I gave up my belief in any external authority that deemed me intrinsically unworthy. Would I be struck by lightning, doomed? Was there in fact a belief system that did not view human beings as victims, *fallen*, failed, evil, or less than, in need of salvation and redemption from themselves? And let's be further clear here: we are not just talking religious or spiritual systems because this theme is endemic in our politics, economics, sciences, gender relations, and more.

Critically, in the liberating deconstruction and overhaul, I came to not only understand that thought creates reality, but that I had the right to create reality on my own terms, and that there was no real *line* to be afraid of crossing except those I had believed to be real. Additionally, I came to understand that the Universe was in fact a friendly place that thrived on expansion, and that expansion or contraction (or happiness or unhappiness for that matter) boiled down to thought.

What freed me so much was physics, string theory, frequency and vibration, a limitless quantum field that responds to our observations, and the knowledge that thought collapses the field's quantum waves into the forms we experience as people, places, emotions, things, and more. Negative thought collapses reality around negativity. Positive thought collapses reality around positivity. Believe in an *us-and-them* world, and you live it. Believe in *wellbeing*, and you live it. Yes, countless mystics and avatars had espoused similar things for millennia, but human interpretation promoted the separation of human beings from their brilliant power to create reality. Whether viewed through lenses or systems (old or new) human beings remained fallen somehow and in need of fixing.

But... what if we were all OK? What if we were all *worthy*, and didn't need fixing?

Research told me we are able to decode only 2,000 bits of 400 billion bits of frequency in every moment, and I wondered what existed beyond 2,000 bits. I wondered just how many realities upon realities existed within all those other billions of bits. And I loved learning that changing one's thoughts (frequencies and vibrations) changed our health, relationships, finances, and more. I loved learning that unless I believed in *lack* or *us-and-them*, they wouldn't be a part of my life. I learned that 80% of our self-talk is negative, and immediately understood the sleeping and waking nightmares we create with that 80%. I learned that we use only 5% of our brains and that western scientists deemed 97% of our DNA to be *junk*, and I wondered about the unused 95% brain-matter and the so-called junk. I learned that we weren't genetically-hardwired for anything at all, and that we have chemicals within ourselves for all states of being, triggered by thought, from unworthiness and depression to passion, joy, appreciation and love. I learned that nothing shows up in your life except by invitation from you via thought, whether from the present or from before you got here. And I learned that when we die, we weren't greeted with judgments and punishment, but with admiration, questions, and wonder.

Importantly, I came to see that everything I had done and everything I was about, centered upon defying and dismantling that *unworthiness* because I wanted to be my own authority; free of cruel standards, beliefs, and interpretations. Knowing that all is possible within a limitless and infinite field, that I have the power to choose, and that unworthiness, punishment, and judgment are based upon the most destructive and false of premises... freed me.

In giving myself permission to live – really live – without fear, I came to feel that passion for life running unhindered through me, and I returned full-circle into my purpose of helping and teaching others. My life had finetuned me in so many incredible ways, but now, there were no crazy hoops to jump through to become worthy before any external authority.

I was sovereign.

I have been exceedingly blessed with great and loving (and not so loving) teachers, family, friends, students, participants, and clients the world over who have journeyed with me in all the stages of my life. And it is to them that I say *thank you* now and express my deepest gratitude.

In sharing parts of my story, it is my intention that you perhaps embrace some of it to free yourself of the inner tyranny of perceived unworthiness. I believe the tyranny will have made you exceptionally courageous, strong, and a seeker of your own truth. But a time will come when you no longer require that unworthiness you scripted. Only then will that catalyze you into your next step, and will you say good-bye to it with loving appreciation. And you shall then live your purpose with passion; your passion with purpose.

My imagined *unworthiness* has been the greatest Gift.

May you recognize your magnificence.

About the Author

Fatima Bacot, the Creating Reality Mentor, specializes in removing pain and suffering by teaching others the secrets to happiness and fulfillment in all areas of their lives. She does this through the mediums of International seminars, speaking, personal mentoring and healing, teleseminars and webinars, her writings, CDs, MP3s, blog, and more.

Fatima provides incisive clarity into the inner workings of one's mind, emotions, body, and psyche, bringing to light stagnant and crippling patterns, and the strategies to move forward. Additionally, she brilliantly presents the big picture of change that is exponentially unfolding globally (and beyond) in contexts that are visionary, illuminating, and practical.

Down-to-earth and empowering, her work dynamically showcases her vast research into numerous global arenas, as part of humanity's current evolutionary trajectory. Fatima lives with her husband on the Gold Coast in Australia. To learn more, please visit her website.

http://www.fatimabacot.com

HOW OPRAH IGNITED MY PASSION

Megan Castran

"So, what is your next goal?" I was asked in a magazine article in 2005, after I had just sold my jewellery pieces to Paul Smith in London.

"I'd like to meet Oprah!" I replied.

Little did I know at that time the amazing series of events that would lead me to actually have Oprah in my house for dinner on her *Australian Ultimate Adventure.*

Oprah inspired me to start a business way back in 1993. I had a one year-old baby and I was a stay-at-home mother. I saw Oprah chatting to women who were in marriages they did not want to be in, but because they had become accustomed to a certain lifestyle they stayed in loveless marriages. I decided then and there that I never wanted to feel like that. Ever. I wanted to be in my marriage because I loved my husband.

I started by hand-painting ceramic plates and personalizing them with children's names and this led to an opportunity to design bed linen. My range ended up selling to all the major stores throughout Australia. However, I now design and hand make jewellery and that is my true passion; that and social media.

The reason I so wanted to meet Oprah was not because of her fame, but because I truly wanted to be able to thank the woman who had ignited the fires of finding my passion and creating a business I love.

So when I went on vacation to Hawaii in 2006 and heard pool-side that Oprah was there with all her staff and their families to celebrate twenty years in television, I could not believe it!

After five days of hoping I would see her, on my last day at the resort I spied her getting her picture taken individually with all the families. There was a huge line and she was about twenty steps away from me. I could *see* her and I could *hear* her.

My heart was racing.

I called out to her when she was having a break. "Hi Oprah from Australia."

I thought that if I did that I might be able to jog her memory if I ever got to go to the Oprah Show. She turned around and gave me a huge wave! Needing no further encouragement I called out, "I started my business thirteen years ago because of you!"

With that, Oprah stood and walked over to me. I was tongue-tied and felt awkward trying to tell her everything I had rehearsed in my head so many times. She was kind and patient and listened to me.

"I have no doubt the success of my marriage is partly due to me having some financial independence," I told her. She was thrilled and gave me a high-five and interlocked her fingers in mine.

"You go girl, and God bless," she said.

With her permission, my daughter Zoe took a quick photo before Oprah returned to her group.

Six months later in January 2007, I was at the Oprah Show in Chicago. All I wanted was for Oprah to ask who had come the furthest distance so I could talk to her again. Guess what her first words were when she entered?

I could not believe it. I raised my hand and called out, "Australia!"

She looked at me and said, "You win."

I asked her if she recalled our meeting and after I jogged her memory, she totally did. She told me that if she ever got to Australia she would call me as I would be the only person she knew! I stood from my seat, walked down to the stage, and handed her my card. She got her photographer to take our picture. As she left the set at the end I saw my card had dropped to the floor. My heart sank. Then Oprah turned around as if reading my mind and said, "Where's that card? I want Megan's card."

I was elated and truly believed that that was not the end of my Oprah experience.

I attended the show during the following three years until 2010. I spoke to her every time, but in 2010 she remembered me fully and told me she still had my card. We joked again about her calling me. Little did I know she had already begun to plan her Australian trip!

When Oprah announced she was coming to Australia I was filled with happiness and when she made a YouTube video saying she was going to look up the people who she had taken the cards from, quoting our conversation, I was beside myself! Could it be possible that Oprah really would call me up?

In the meantime an American friend of mine introduced me to a friend of hers via Facebook: Carrie Abbott. Carrie was one of the *Oprah Ultimate Viewers* who had been chosen for the trip to Australia. We instantly liked each other and chatted regularly on Skype. She told me she had been following an Aussie fashion blogger, Karen Cheng, for ages. Karen agreed to *style* Carrie for the Oprah Sydney Show and I told Carrie I would make her a necklace. We could not wait to meet.

So when I received a call from Harpo asking if I would host a taco night for ten of their *Ultimate Viewers*, of course I said yes. I was thrilled they had seen the article written by Suzanne Carbone in *The Age* newspaper and I was excited to be having some association with the Oprah Aussie trip. Taco night has been going on for twenty years at our house so it was not hard to choose who my fourteen guests would be. It would be my loyal taco night crew.

I swung into top gear organizing beautiful wines from TarraWarra Estate in the Yarra Valley, gorgeous De Bortoli Dessert wines, an amazing cake from a dear friend Christopher – *The Cake Man* – and flowers from Domain Flowers. I knew that it would need to be presented well as my family would be representing Australians overseas and I wanted the American guests to have a great night.

When the doorbell rang on December 10th, 2010 and I opened it expecting to see the ten American guests, I could not believe my eyes. Instead, there was Oprah herself smiling in front of me with two fabulous bottles of tequila. In fact, I still looked around for the other guests, but she told me it was only her!

Oprah was amazing from the minute she entered my home. She was neither intimidating nor intimidated. She was a fun, friendly, engaging woman who had us all laughing and dancing and sipping margaritas.

I had organized two awesome musicians, Paris Zachariou, who had her singing instantly followed by Ross Wilson singing his Aussie classic *Eaglerock*. Oprah loved them so much she flew them both to Sydney to warm up the audiences for her shows. It was incredible how she continued to give opportunities when she could. She also flew the whole taco group to Sydney to attend the Oprah House show.

Before Oprah left my home she made a YouTube video with me for my Jewelchic channel talking about my vision board that had a picture of her on it with the words: "I'm On My Way." Every time I look at that video I am just filled with joy and gratitude as I had made a video in 2008 saying how I didn't know why, but I thought it was not impossible that Oprah could come to my house and make a video with me! This is truly the power of positive thought.

At the last minute a private jet company, Southern Cross Jets, offered to fly us all up on their new Gulfstream 450 as an incredible treat! Our Oprah week just kept getting better and better.

So in Sydney I met my gorgeous American friend, Carrie, and my taco friends, and I sat three rows from the front at the show taping. When the show finished we were ushered backstage for another chat with Oprah and a photograph.

Then in January I was lucky enough to be in the USA and attended a taping of the Oprah Show about happiness. It was so great to see her again so soon after our adventure. She talked about experiences being a great gift of happiness and I can honestly say that the memories from that taco night will last for a lifetime. It has also made my friends from YouTube around the world happy too. One teacher in Amsterdam showed her students our video and they all made vision boards in class, others have come to realize that we can indeed create our dreams. The taco night has sent ripples of happiness around the world.

So what has Oprah taught me? She has taught me to find the best in people, to encourage positivity, to enjoy life and to help others, to be *connected* to this world and to truly, intrinsically believe that *anything* is possible. We are all the same. Some are doctors, some are trades-people, and some are stay-at-home parents, but we are all the same. Look beyond the outer package.

Everyone has a story.

About the Author

Megan Castran is best known for her jewellery business and is a walking advertisement for her trinkets. She's also a dedicated YouTuber, filing online video reports under the name Jewelchic from red carpet events to taco nights with friends.

Without setting out to be, the gal with the grin has become a self-help guru, inspiring those who need inspiration with her regular Saturday videos chatting about life, love, and happiness with her husband, Paul. She has also become passionate about musical theatre and interviews stars around the world from their various shows.

http://www.jewelchic.com

PURSUING POTENTIAL

Dennis Andrew

I remember seeing a tactical martial artist in his early twenties, dressed in a brown button-down shirt, blue jeans, and flip flops. As I stared at my reflection, I was trying to create possibilities of how I was ever going to succeed.

Very recently, I walked into a room to find my best friend dead. I remember feeling my heart freeze. At the same time, the woman I loved was with someone else and the misinterpretations were deteriorating my spirit. Life meant nothing anymore.

My story begins from the very bottom.

A major part of my martial arts training was in understanding human behavior. I needed to analyze people in a way that would allow me to recognize threats in a given area, with only a quick scan. In this time, I was to understand and accurately portray their process of thought and most likely path of action.

As I became more involved with behavior research and neuroscience, I learned some very interesting facts about what happens in your brain *while you are on the journey* to achieving a goal. Developing a solution causes a chemical reaction in the brain that simulates the feelings of achievement. Because it is so satisfying, most people get stuck within the euphoria of the passion, and don't take proper action toward its attainment.

In martial arts, if you want to reach a certain skill level, you need to be conditioned for it. This process is difficult from start to finish. Ultimately, conditioning brings to light *when* you have the sufficient strength, skill, and understanding of responsibility for your goal. The difficulties point directly to the areas that presently need some work.

If you give up before the process is complete, you are either not ready for your goal, or you don't want it badly enough. If you don't give up, you will be conditioned right *into* the achievement of that goal.

To be quite frank, I hated school. Nevertheless, I graduated with a 4.0 grade point average at the age of sixteen. I was driven by my desire to end my scholastic torture. By eighteen, I had a decent job as an electromechanical and pneumatics engineer. Soon, I was put in charge of the department. Although I did well, it soon occurred to me that I was being paid what someone else thought I was worth; that I was essentially trading a portion of my life for their price. I realized that we really do trade our lives for what we do, and it was time for me to trade it for values I wanted. I left the field, determined never to return.

It was 4:40 a.m. several years later, and my alarm told me it was time to take my morning run. Despite my distaste for running, I was instantly awakened because I was living in my truck and the temperature was only ten degrees Fahrenheit outside. This was a cold winter in Copley, Ohio. Breakfast consisted of two granola bars or a pack of cheese crackers. I had to discipline myself by setting aside twelve crackers a day because I didn't know if I would be able to buy food for the day. Each night, I stayed in a warm building for as late as I could.

I had come to this condition because my family and I didn't see eye to eye on my pursuits. I was working on creating a company that would later play a huge role in business development, specifically by targeting the science of how a client's brain works in the buying process. Financially, things were not appearing to take shape. I was assumed to be on the wrong track, and I had failed many times in the past.

I was often told that it wasn't *working out* because I wasn't doing what I was *supposed to be doing*, which was to get a job. An ultimatum was put up where I would either do things as my family saw fit, or I would need to leave. I chose the latter without hesitation. I had learned too much to be able to go back, but obviously there were quite a few things I still needed to learn.

The pieces to my passions were developed over time, and they were completely unrelated to the words on my resume. I soon understood that my purpose was incorrectly judged by those who thought they knew me and it sure as life didn't polish easily. I wouldn't tell others about my living condition for fear that I might actually consider what I was saying, and would become too discouraged to maintain my drive to succeed. In fact, I dressed better, and all the more surrounded myself with those who were successful.

It was tough, and the trained side of me was looking for a lesson. I knew my circumstances were really testing whatever skills or qualities were missing, but I thought I was looking for tangible deficiencies. The skills turned out to be character traits, like gratitude, stability, focus, perseverance, faith, and open-mindedness. These definitely weren't the lessons I thought I needed. I thought I felt a greater physical lack, like some sort of marketing tactic was missing. But all of those qualities had strengthened and purified my mindset, which then uncovered the tangible deficiencies I wouldn't have been able to correct otherwise.

While learning those skills, I had come to terms with myself: with my condition, heartaches, love, discomfort, lack, fears, and potential. I learned that worrying is like a prayer for things we don't want, and that the Law of Attraction was just a scientific synonym for faith. I learned that prayer has little to do with what we say or how we say it, and everything to do with what we believe and live. I learned that we really do have things according to our own beliefs and that our faith is either in something, in its variant, or in its opposite.

The quality of our life precisely reflects where our faith lies.

This made my living condition more bearable. The mere thought of getting a job made me feel like a failure. But worse than that, I knew that if I had a job and things weren't working out with my concurrent business endeavors, I'd be less pressed to keep trying because a paycheck would be coming. I then decided not to eat until I earned some sort of income from what I was pursuing. This was like being the donkey *and* the farmer.

People would see me on my laptop, drinking coffee every day. Most of them thought they were looking at a successful businessman. They didn't know that later that night I'd be in three pairs of pants sleeping in the bitter cold. Deep inside, I felt rejected because of my goals, and it's a lonely road. It was probably one of the best places in my life because I learned not to form my life by others' opinions or expectations of me. If there was something I was going to do, I learned to do it sincerely without caring if another accepted it. This... was contrary to my nature.

The young, beautiful woman that I loved meant so much to me, that a mere thought of her would give me the courage to move forward. We couldn't communicate. In a notepad, I would write a letter to her each night summarizing my day. I did it because it made me feel as though she could hear me. I felt like she believed in me more than anyone else. I had a few friends that believed in me as well. Some challenged me to different ways of thinking, and some just loved me for who I was. They were fascinated by my enthusiasm for my endeavors, and I felt valued by them. My future was shaped with these individuals in mind.

The feelings of disappointment became stale to me and I was annoyed by them. Daily I exercised my mind by visualizations and meditation. Because I had a passion for understanding the mind, I was like a sponge for any relative information. I did a lot of work without compensation in an effort to prove the effectiveness of properly converting this information into tangible applications. I believed in what I was doing and aimed at building reputation.

My focus was on quality and long term payoff. In several years, I wanted to be able to look every one of my clients in the eye, confident that I had given them the best that I had, and that they remained happy with the results.

Money started coming, slowly at first and in spurts. I was getting comfortable living in my truck, which was not good. This was the work of the *psycho-cybernetic mechanism*, a mechanism in the brain designed for the body's safety. It works like a thermostat, and in this instance, it was programming my current living condition to be recognized as *normal*. To counter it, I raised my standard of living.

I was unaware that people were recommending my work, and my company's reputation was spreading. Clients started seeking my expertise, resulting in a much stronger income. This was the first time I felt rewarded for sticking through the heat. To my great satisfaction, I was contacted by several prominent individuals that had heard of my work and commended me for it. Certain clients were telling me I had changed their lives.

Until this point, I had experienced a lot of loss, disappointment, and heartbreak. It only occurred to me later, that these experiences were the very conditioning I needed to be able to connect with others. After all, I was in the business of understanding people at an emotional level. This was the beginning of NNOS Studios, a now incredibly effective business development company that incorporates neuromarketing applications and market research, to quickly tap into the client's mind.

I have an extreme passion for business and an interest in the path less travelled. This comes at a heavy price. Sometimes you lose everything while trying to attain your goals, so it pays to be sure you believe in them. I remember feeding off sayings like: "You won't be led this far just to have the rug pulled out from under you." But I've also learned to ignore the friends and relatives who tried to get me to walk off the rug. Taking their advice would probably give me their results, and that wasn't my idea of success. This was very difficult to do because some of them had given me very valuable support at the beginning of my efforts.

Entrepreneurs have different mentalities than victims. The victim is always at the effect of a cause; the entrepreneur always finds himself at the cause of an effect. The one lets you off the hook, and the other forces you to think. The victim's mind is comfortable; the entrepreneur's is not.

The road was painful, cold, emotionally exhausting, filled with hunger, and littered with failure. But I stuck through it. I refused to break down. Although I directed much of my passion to helping other businesses succeed, I have gone on to establish several businesses of my own.

I've established The Weathered Rock, a specialty landscaping company, because I have experience in the field and genuinely enjoy it. I've formed two businesses with one of my closest friends. One is a real estate investment firm, and the other is Coffee Cave, an incredibly unique and accommodating coffee shop.

Another company that I developed was spawned by two extremes: love and hate. It is an intelligence agency created to combat human trafficking. This company vision was designed so that together with several highly trained operatives, we can rescue and help those that are less fortunate. It is an operation where I can go whole-heartedly, even when my heart is in pieces.

With every new endeavor come large challenges, the mother of perfected inventions. But I've learned that you fail your way to achievement... if the dream within you sings louder than the logic that tells you it's smarter to give up. Many have great passions. But a great passion with no action is like a huge fish with no tail.

Challenges are the entrepreneur's stepping stones – invitations to take immediate action. They are not to be discouraging, but empowering. Take a look at the stone ahead of you, step on it, catch your balance, and then look to the next one.

About the Author

Dennis is a highly motivated entrepreneur from Ohio that finds a purpose in the pursuit of potential. He particularly enjoys the subconscious territories, swims against the tide, and chooses the road less travelled.

His adventurous spirit has taken his career from a professional engineer into extremely unique territories within the business world. He judges the greatness of an accomplishment by the size of the odds against it.

As an entrepreneur, Dennis has founded or partnered in over six successful ventures in the last four years. He believes in generosity, and has spent countless hours helping others improve their businesses and lives, often without compensation. His business efforts are found in his company, NNOS Studios.

The paradigm by which he lives is defined by the basic character of justice: You reap what you sow.

http://www.nnosstudios.com

BIRTHING A R-EVOLUTION

Lynne Thorsen

I discovered my *passion* for empowered and ecstatic birth during the birth of my first child in November 2001. Ten years later, I realized that healing and empowering birth is also my *purpose* for this lifetime.

This story begins many years before, when during a class at school I watched Frederick Leboyer's Birth Without Violence. I remember deciding then, that if I had a baby, I wanted to give birth in this non-interventionist, calm, and loving manner. Years later, I read Michael Domeyko Roland's *Absolute Happiness*. In it, he wrote a chapter about birth and how important the process of natural birth is to preparing the being for a contented life in the physical realm. In addition, a chronic childhood illness and a major knee operation in my teens caused me to develop a dislike of hospitals and a general distrust of the medical profession.

After I married and we decided we wanted to start a family, I read Christiane Northrup's *Women's Bodies, Women's Wisdom* and once again, I found her chapter on pregnancy and birth reinforcing my ideas that our current method of birthing in hospitals with doctors, machines, and drugs was not ideal. This and my background conditioning made it easy to decide then and there that I wanted a homebirth. I asked my husband to read the chapter and support me in this decision. He did and he did!

A few months later, I discovered I was pregnant. We were living in the UK and homebirth is well supported by the National Health Service. We signed up for the community midwife program and everything was perfect.

Thirty-two weeks into pregnancy, my whole world was rocked when the midwife, during a prenatal check, declared that my baby is breech: positioned in the uterus so that the buttocks or feet must be delivered first. She declared that if it stays breech we would be unable to have a homebirth. I reeled with shock and realized *just* how committed I was to birthing my baby at home. The thought of going to the hospital, and most likely having a caesarean, was completely abhorrent to me.

I researched everything I could about breech birth. The medical policy in most developed countries is to recommend caesarean section for breech presentation. I discovered that the basis for this is a thirty year-old Canadian research paper, seriously flawed in its design and conclusions. This only encouraged me to continue my quest for a homebirth.

We tried some natural methods for turning the baby inside the uterus and when all else failed, we hired two independent midwives. They requested that I have a late scan at the hospital, to determine both the size and position of the baby. The trainee obstetrician that gave me the results proceeded to lecture me on my choice to birth at home and finally laid down his trump card: "Well if you want to risk the life of your unborn child…"

My rage erupted and I stormed out, determined not to return. I knew deep inside that I had more knowledge about natural breech birth than he did. Maybe he did me a favor, as I put the energy of that rage to positive use during the birth.

It was difficult to stay true to my conviction when birth was such an unknown to me. However, I gritted my teeth in the face of opposition and stayed positive. Meanwhile, I did everything I could to physically, mentally, and spiritually prepare for labor and birth. I practiced guided visualizations, meditation, and perineal massage. I drank raspberry leaf tea, ate a healthy diet, and exercised regularly. Weekly, I attended prenatal yoga and birth-preparation classes.

I went into labor on my due date and everything progressed like clockwork. My beautiful baby girl was born in the comfort of my own home… with no pain, drugs, stitches, or intervention. At no stage did I feel the need to ask for pain-relief. My support team was wonderful and I found it easy to stay focussed and committed.

I had birthed outside the normal paradigm and most importantly, I had avoided a caesarean section. I was in charge of my own domain and I created the ambience that I wanted, and no one made me do anything I didn't want to. An hour after the birth, I relaxed in a lovely warm bath with my baby. Several hours later we all toasted our triumph with a glass of champagne.

I was ecstatic and empowered!

My daughter's birth was a complete and utter success. It made me realize that many women were suffering unnecessary intervention and surgery and missing out on the opportunity to experience the power and joy of uninterrupted, natural birth.

In the weeks after the birth, I attended several mother's group coffee-mornings and listened to the other women eagerly giving accounts of their births. Their stories were full of trauma, pain, humiliation, and disappointment, and I felt that there was no place for me to speak of the wonderful, empowering, and joyous experience that we had had. This created a great sadness in me and a deep desire to tell the world it doesn't have to be that way; *we* can be in charge; *we* can birth our babies in joy and ecstasy.

It seemed incredulous that strong, successful women believed they *couldn't do it* when it came to birth. Many gave up the opportunity to experience their inner strength and access their sacred inner wisdom. I felt frustrated by a society and culture that actively encouraged this disempowerment and felt angry with those who chose to profit financially from the *business* of birth.

My education about birth continued with my subsequent children. My second child was born underwater at home in Australia. This birth taught me the importance of a safe environment and having the freedom to move, breathe, and verbalize at will. I was at a friend's place during early labor and instinctively didn't feel safe or uninhibited to go into my primal self. The contractions I experienced in the car on the way home were the most intense and painful that I had experienced thus far, as I wasn't free to move around and breathe deeply.

My Australian midwife was wonderful, supporting me from the edge of the pool as I birthed him myself. He lay in my arms, completely at peace, not breathing, and wonderfully calm. In his own time, he gently came into his body and started to breathe. Later, my husband cut the cord and my two year-old daughter entered the water to welcome her baby brother.

My third child's birth taught me about the value of trust and support. Also, for the first time, I experienced the negative impact of intervention. By this stage, we were dividing our time between Australia and France, where birth is highly medical and home-birth is not very common in the latter.

We eventually located a midwife, an hour-and-a-half-hour-drive from our home. We only had two prenatal meetings and we didn't establish the necessary trust or bond needed. She *insisted* on internal examinations and her requirements for the birth were more medical. I felt uneasy. Due to the language barrier and distance, my experienced support team of my husband and mother also felt the same.

When labor stalled after several hours, my midwife suggested breaking my waters. My lack of trust in her, my support team and myself eventually led me to agree and taught me how easily it is to be persuaded to accept unnecessary interventions. What I needed most was someone to look me deeply in the eyes and tell me that I could do it and to trust in the wonderful process of birth.

This kind of support was not available to me during this birth.

Breaking the waters caused labor to intensify and become painful. My third child was born in a rush. His face was blue, with the cord around his neck. At the time, everyone believed the intervention was necessary to prevent a disaster. I disagreed. I believe the intervention caused the cord to entangle around his neck and endanger his life. He wanted and needed more time and I didn't have enough trust to go deep inside myself to talk to him and give him what he needed. Although delighted with my son, the birth left me with feelings of disappointment and negative self-judgment.

My passion for birth contracted over the following years and so did my sense of worth and purpose. When I experienced a deep existential crisis four years later, I knew that I had lost any sense of who I was or why I was here. I had achieved many things: career, loving relationship, motherhood, and travelling the world. Yet something was missing.

I realized I needed to discover my *true* purpose.

I discovered the work of Binnie A. Dansby and immediately resonated with her passion for ecstatic, empowered birth. It brought me back to the passion I had experienced all those years ago. I joined her SOURCE Process & Breathwork training in Estonia and was amazed that the angel card I received at the beginning of the training year was purpose.

Perfect!

Although I was extremely comfortable around the subject of birth, I experienced a physical and psychological contraction whenever I had to consider my own birth, even though I had no conscious knowledge of it. It became apparent that the story of my own birth held the key to successfully being able to live my purpose. After peeling off many layers and working hard on my own healing, I eventually remembered my birth. It was my Source experience of change and I became aware of the limiting decisions I made in those first moments. Through a process of forgiveness, I was able to release those negative thoughts so that they no longer influenced who I am!

The shift in my own consciousness was so significant that I realized I wanted to help inspire others to do the same.

We each share the universality of the birth experience and the individuation of our own birth stories. Healing birth is the same as healing life.

> "The quality of birth affects the quality of life, and in turn, impacts and shapes the quality of society. Birth is the Source experience in the body and we were conscious at birth. Thus our birth affects our whole subsequent mental, emotional and spiritual well being. The decisions we make at birth are the foundation for the beliefs and patterns that are active in our lives. Those individual attitudes and patterns translate to the attitudes and patterns displayed by nations." –Binnie A Dansby, 1989

My passion and my purpose have two equally important aspects:

- Healing birth in order to heal life.

- Empowering birth so that future generations can enter the world and go forth in joy and ecstasy.

I am passionate about inspiring people to connect to their inner wisdom and heal their birth stories, allowing them to evolve their consciousness from life-diminishing thoughts to life-enhancing ones.

I am passionate about empowering women and their partners to step outside the prevailing cultural beliefs and to learn the truth about birth; to realize they can be in charge and trust the process of natural, ecstatic birth.

I am currently co-writing a book with my mentor and teacher, Binnie A Dansby. Our intention is to inspire, empower, and create an R-Evolution in birth consciousness so that ecstatic birth is the *new* consciousness for birth, the world over,

It is time!

About the Author

Lynne is a qualified holistic therapist in Integrated Self Empowerment Therapy (ISET) and is currently completing her training in SOURCE therapeutic breathwork in Estonia. Previously, she enjoyed a diverse set of careers in physical education, hospitality management, and travel.

Lynne was born in Melbourne, Australia, and now lives in south west France with her husband and three children.

She has lived abroad in the UK, France, and the USA, travelled extensively all over the world and still calls Australia home!

Lynne's great passion and purpose is *revolution of birth consciousness* and she is working on several projects to increase awareness in this area, including her first book, a blogspot, and an empowering birth program. Her three children were all born at home in three different countries: UK, Australia, and France.

Her website offers more about her journey and her passion of *creating ecstatic birth*.

http://www.lynnethorsen.com

WHEN I GROW UP

Lisa G. Jing

Every kid wonders what they'll be when they grow up. It's the customary question an adult asks when meeting a child for the first time. For as long as I can remember, the notion of vocation or profession has intrigued me. Seems that the fascination with occupation runs deep in our culture as well, based on the popular adult conversation-starter, "What do you do for a living?"

When I was eight, I fantasized about being a famous actress performing on stage or in the movies. I knew the lines from the popular commercials of that era and revelled in reciting all of them from memory. Though I didn't become a child actress, I did indulge that dream a bit by earning a spot on the cheerleading squad and winning the most valuable cheerleader award in my rookie year.

In middle school, I dreamt of being a musician and singer spreading important messages through memorable melodies and thought-provoking lyrics which I heard so much on the radio in those days.

Then reality set in.

Despite private guitar lessons and countless hours blissfully singing along to my favorite ballads on LPs and 45s, no one was going to invite me to join the choir. To this day, I'm still baffled how someone can love music as much as I do and yet be completely bereft of any musical talent. A terrible injustice indeed!

By the time I was in high school, my inner nerd had emerged and I contemplated being a scientist satisfying my endless curiosity and unlocking the mysteries of nature. It was not until the weighty math requirements and the prospect of spending my days in a white lab coat that this dream was put to rest.

Throughout my childhood and adolescent years, the question of *what do I want to be when I grow up?* continued to plague me. I was no closer to an answer when the time came for me to apply to college. I loved to learn. I loved to learn about... *everything*, and I was a straight-A student, so there was no clear indication of where I might focus my studies. The immensity of possibilities was so overwhelming to me that I opted for community college, where I'd have two years of general education to figure it out.

I enjoyed all the college level courses, but by Fall of my sophomore year, I was still no closer to finding my path. My career quandary was now a serious challenge, as I had to declare a major in order to transfer to a four-year university. I ended up staying an additional year at the community college because I just couldn't choose. Alas, I finally decided to major in psychology which gave me the chance to delve into the mystery of human behavior and perhaps finally figure out what made people (mainly myself) tick.

Turned out that the world of work provided some of the best clues about what I'm good at and the kind of work I most enjoy.

During my senior year in high school, my first job was selling clothing in a boutique for petit women. It was cool being a teenage girl immersed in fashions that I loved, but after only three days I decided to leave. I simply couldn't tell people that they looked good when they didn't, just to make a sale. I realized that I have to feel good about the work I do.

I tried retail a couple more times. I was a cashier at a sporting goods store where I enjoyed meeting the variety of people who came in seeking equipment for their favorite pastimes. A year later, I worked for an upscale wine and liquor merchant and was saddened to see the regulars come in for their daily fix of alcohol and cigarettes. It really bothered me that I was stocking the shelves that supplied their unhealthy habits.

Shortly after college, I got married and had my first child. I continued on to graduate school with the plan that I would become a marriage, family, and child therapist. I was captivated with the study of human behavior and I thought helping people with their personal challenges would sustain me.

I worked my way through graduate school as the front office manager of a dental practice. I chose the job for very practical reasons: the hours allowed me to work full-time and attend classes at night while raising my newborn son and maintaining a household. I did what I thought I had to do to meet all my obligations. Truth is, I hated that job. It didn't suit me at all. I just wasn't cut out for an administrative position. I was so miserable at that job that I used to cry in the bathroom at lunchtime.

It was pathetic.

When I finally completed graduate school, I left the dental office and got a job doing intake evaluations and admissions for a psychiatric and chemical dependency hospital. At last I got to apply what I learned in college and grad school. I conducted suicide interventions and helped people in crises, which I was really good at. I found the work deeply meaningful and fulfilling and decided that from then on, the work I do has to resonate with my values and make a real contribution to the world.

An attractive opportunity for my husband as a result of the high-tech boom prompted an unexpected relocation of our family from Southern California to Silicon Valley in the northern half of the state. In the process, my career was seemingly sidetracked. I was unable to find an equivalent position in a hospital in our new location. So I decided to venture into the world of healthcare marketing to learn how to build my practice someday as a family therapist, which is something they don't teach in grad school. In the same setting where I once did clinical intakes, I was now responsible for assessing the facility's competitive position. The same diagnostic and treatment planning skills I used as a clinician, I now applied to market analyses and strategic marketing plans.

The more I learned about business, the more excited I became about my career. I gradually came to realize that although I found the clinical work interesting and rewarding in many ways, I didn't consider it fun. I recognized that whatever work I do, I have to *truly* enjoy it.

I then made a bold decision to change career paths and focus on the world of marketing.

Over the next several years, I held increasingly responsible marketing positions for a variety of healthcare providers. I became fascinated with what makes some companies or organizations successful while others flounder. I noticed that teams that share a common vision and purpose tend to be more successful and a lot more fun to work in.

After a few years, the allure of Silicon Valley, with its many perks and continuous innovation, convinced me to change industries. Leaving the healthcare world behind, I jumped on the high-tech bandwagon and became a technical recruiter with a world-leading technology company. There, I applied all my previous experience as a clinician and marketer to assessing candidates and matching people to opportunities. And as a recruiter, I played a key role in working with managers to help them build their teams. I was surprised by how much I loved it and by how quickly I flourished in the fast-paced business world.

Around the same time, I was exposed to a number of great training programs offered by the company I worked for. My passion for learning was reignited and I eagerly consumed as many workshops, seminars, and DVDs as I could. During my daily commute, my car became a mobile classroom with an extensive curriculum of CDs on leadership, personal development, and success in business.

It became apparent to me that my career was much more than just finding satisfying work that pays a sufficient wage to meet my survival needs. My chosen profession is an expression of my larger mission and life purpose; my reason for being on the planet at this time and place in history.

How I use my time and talents is my unique contribution while I'm here.

After the infamous dotcom bust in 2000, my career took yet another turn. The company focus quickly switched from hiring people to building an organizational culture that could flex and endure and adapt to sudden changes in the market in the long run. Over the next several years I was a founding core team member of several initiatives related to corporate culture in executive development, inclusion and diversity, and employee health. I discovered that each of these areas is critical to creating a positive environment where people can be their best and passionately enjoy what they're doing.

I'm now the founder of my own company whose mission is to transform the workplace into an environment where people are their whole and best selves. My long-held dream to be on stage is being fulfilled as a speaker and trainer in the area of organizational transformation. My desire to share an important message is manifesting as I speak on the critical role that passion at work plays in helping workers be healthier and happier in their jobs while maximizing the company's overall success.

My inner nerd gets to demonstrate through data how healthy lifestyle practices and intrinsic motivation are the most effective strategies for keeping organizations vital and thriving. My emphasis is on life balance for both mental health and business success. I'm actively marketing my message to get it out to the business world and… I'm having a blast doing all of this.

I finally found the message and the meaning for my career and life. Seems my career has come full circle. Every job, every skill, every experience I've had throughout my life as a clinician, marketer, recruiter, parent, human resource professional, trainer, consultant, and entrepreneur is essential to what I'm doing now. I'm finally clear on what I want to be when I grow up!

Throughout my life, I've had the sense that I was being called to something greater. Each step along the journey has built upon the previous one, requiring me to be more and more of who I am. The more I accept and embrace the calling, the happier and more fulfilled I become.

And so the journey continues…

About the Author

Lisa Jing is the founder and CEO of Synergy at Work, a training and consulting firm, whose mission is to transform the workplace into an environment where people are their whole and best selves.

Prior to starting her own company, Lisa was recognized as a thought leader in integrated health solutions in the corporate sector. Lisa was senior program manager on Cisco's Global Health Engagement team where she developed strategies and implemented programs to enhance the well-being of employees and their families.

Her passion is to bring more spirit to the workplace through organizational culture change and ground-breaking programs which foster integration of mind, body, and spirit.

Lisa holds an M.A. in counselling psychology from Loyola Marymount University and a B.A. in psychology from the University of California, San Diego. Her career portfolio includes clinical counselling, healthcare marketing, technical recruiting, and human resources.

http://www.lisagjing.com/

THE GOLDEN THREAD OF PASSION

Lynden Boehm

In his book, *The Passion Plan*, Richard Chang says:

> "*My passion has been a thread weaving through my life, into and out of activities, across experiences, and through the years. We all have such threads of passion, and they remain with us, sometimes on the surface and sometimes woven deep in our fabric, waiting to re-emerge at a later date. Passioneers capture these threads over time and use them to create beautiful designs. Others allow them to become torn or frayed or lose sight of them altogether.*"

I firmly believe your passion and purpose are all woven in that golden thread; they are intertwined and your childhood dreams are often very clear indicators of so. I pick up my thread at my first memory of what I wanted to be as a child. I remember getting a nurse's outfit for my 6th birthday, which I loved wearing, pretending to be a nurse to the farm dogs and pet lambs and my dolls.

After a stint in the hospital I realized what nurses *really* do, and I wasn't so excited anymore about blood and guts, or about giving needles and cleaning bed pans. When I look at my subsequent careers in hospitality, massage, and party-plan selling, I see my golden thread weaving through; helping people and making them better.

When I was a teenager, I wanted to be a social or youth worker. I didn't do well enough in school to get into university to study that, and enrolled in a totally unsuitable course that led me nowhere. Hence I dropped out of college at twenty-one and I fell into hospitality. I had applied for many jobs to no avail before seeing an advertisement for a bartending school. This involved a week of tuition to be able to serve drinks and run a bar. Feeling I had nothing to lose, I embarked on my hospitality career. I had a lot of fun working in bars and did it well.

A couple of years later, I felt unsettled as I didn't want to be pulling beer for the rest of my life. A stroke of synchronicity occurred when a friend told me that a new hotel management school was opening up in her state. I applied, was accepted, and moved interstate. A new chapter of my life opened up as I learned the intricate details of running a hotel; from making beds to business law.

Upon graduating, I took on various positions around Australia, finally finding my niche in organizing weddings and conferences. I built a strong rapport with my clients as we worked together toward having a successful function. I loved the detail and planning, and the building of relationships with customers.

The hours were very antisocial. I was thirty-five and realized that I was very successfully building other people's businesses and making them a very neat profit. My requests to be paid what I was worth fell on deaf ears, and I felt as if my soul was crying out, "And what about me?!"

It was time to move on.

After leaving the mayhem of hospitality, I got a nine-to-five sales job and I had a life again: time to do things in the evening and have my weekends free! One of the first things I did was enroll into a massage-training course, and I felt like I was home.

There was such a strong pull for me to massage more. I just *had* to do this, and as this new passion overtook my daytime job, it was time to let the security go and follow my heart. Little by little, I built my practice through referrals, working from my home in Sydney. Here I was, at thirty-five, with a brand new career and passion in life; massaging and helping people to be their best by looking after their physical and emotional wellbeing.

In order to support myself in these fledgling stages, I started selling Tupperware. After attending my first Tupperware party at this time and watching my demonstrator, I thought, "I could do this."

And I did!

I excelled at this new *fun* way of making ends meet. Once again, it was building strong personal relationships with my clients, having fun, and improving people's lives, only this time by teaching them to safely and efficiently store their food.

After successfully building my practice in Sydney for seven years, I met my man and, to be with him, I took the leap to moving interstate again. I knew I would build my massage business again, as I loved it so much. The reality was that when I got to Adelaide I knew one other person: my beautiful sister, which was not enough to build a massage practice. So I went back to providing a hospitality service once again, which enabled me to meet people and to adjust to my new relationship and city.

I took on a role as banquet manager and in two years managed to transform their five conference-room business from having an occasional booking to being booked solid. Within six months I needed an assistant and we both worked long and hard in filling those rooms. I loved the business, the relationships, and that sense of satisfaction of a job very well done. Once again, my request for remuneration for my value and the hours I devoted was flatly denied... and my fingers were starting to twitch again. I knew it was time to do what I was really passionate about again: massaging.

By this stage I was forty-five and not at all phased by the fact that most people would consider folding up their massage table at this age! Not me. I was excited and rearing to go, and created mind-maps and vision boards about what I wanted my new business to be like. I found a couple of rooms in an old house close to the center of the city. Bingo! I was in business.

I joined a weekly networking group, which provided me with what essentially became my sales team. As this was my second stint at business building, I had lots of systems in place to make sure I had a profitable and successful business. I also started to use greeting cards to further my relationship with my clients.

What I wanted was my own space to work from. This is when I asked one of my clients, who owned a few cottages nearby, if he had one that would be suitable for me to work from. Another client was an interior designer and we devised a beautiful color scheme of purple and yellow. Another woman I met made a stunning mosaic of my logo, resembling a hand, which hung at the front door. She also taught mosaics so I picked up a new hobby and passion. This practice grew and thrived to the stage where I was fully booked six weeks in advance and had a waiting-list every day.

But change was looming. My partner's work was closing down in that state and the company was very keen to re-locate him to their Melbourne office. There were many deciding factors for us. The main ones being that my thumbs were getting sore and that my dad had been diagnosed with liver cancer, which we figured that in a few months he would need a lot of help. I got all my financial records up to date so that I could put my business on the market... and sold it!

The buyer was a former client, who had been inspired by me to study massage, and wanted to move back to Adelaide: a perfect opportunity for both of us. She moved into the cottage and my clients just slotted in to the new hands that were now massaging them. It was a true win-win situation for everyone. I felt truly blessed to be able to sell my practice and for my clients to have a seamless transition.

I helped my siblings to care for our dad until he passed away, only three months after moving to Melbourne. Then I was left with, "What am I going to do now?" I was fifty-three, had sore thumbs, and knew I couldn't massage again. *So now what?* I am very pleased to report that I didn't even contemplate going back to a hospitality-providing business! I had learned my lesson.

Just before leaving Adelaide I was introduced to microfiber cloths. I loved their environmental impact, which sat well with my values and so I decided to take on selling them by party-plan. There was a major drawback though: I didn't know many people in my new city, but I *knew* I would succeed. Someone suggested I join BNI, which I did, as I saw it as the perfect way to grow my business and meet people. I have since taken on a role within BNI and I now mentor chapters to empower them to be their best and to grow and flourish.

I was successful with this business but not *passionate* about it. That restless feeling of *making a difference but not touching people's hearts* emerged once again. I had been introduced to a network marketing company that allowed me to keep in touch with my customers using greeting cards.

And a new passion was born.

It was a far superior system to the manual method I used in my massage business, where I used to print them up on my computer, fold them, pencil in the date I needed to send them, and put the stamp on. The new system did it all for me. I loved it! It was creative, fun, and efficient. Most importantly I was able to touch people in a way I had never been able to do, as I was often being told, through tears, what an impact receiving a card made. There's that golden thread again right there: helping people and making them better!

Throughout my life there had been a dragging undercurrent of: What is my life's purpose? What am I passionate about? I was expecting bells and whistles. I thought it would be obvious and once you found it, it would never waver or wane. That was until I came across The Passion Test last year. By doing this very simple and profound test I discovered my five top passions. Wow! That was exciting and freeing!

I also discovered that it was about all aspects of you, not just your work-life. I realized that I was just fine the way that I was, that my successes came from being natural and happy, and from following my passions and dreams. It also came from being prepared to give anything a go. Most importantly success is not about the amount of money you have in the bank, or the titles you have; it is about the imprint you leave on someone else's soul.

Another thing I have found is that you need coaches and mentors to support you in your life and your business. Finding a trained facilitator to take me through The Passion Test was amazing and inspired me to do the training too. I also have other coaches as well and the current one is helping me piece together my golden threads and weave this beautiful tapestry of my life. I am super excited that I am, at fifty-seven, about to embark on what feels like the culmination of *all* that I have done in my life, and wrapping my passions and gifts around it as I begin to launch Beaming Enterprises.

About the Author

Lynden Boehm, founder of Beaming Enterprises, assists service-based businesses become more profitable by helping them connect with their clients to create lasting relationships. A natural teacher and facilitator, she provides the owners with the tools to implement these ideas in a systemized way in achieving results.

Beaming Enterprises is a culmination of her gifts, which is a love of business and connecting deeply with people. Her experience has come from twelve years as a banquet manager, successfully building others businesses, then at age thirty-five learning remedial massage. Lynden built thriving practices from scratch in Sydney and Adelaide, with just the connections she made and her knack for relationship marketing.

Lynden now uses her gifts to help businesses make an impact with their clients and is doing what she loves. She is a testament that you can begin to make your true gift shine at any age.

http://www.beamingenterprises.com.au

JUST DO IT!

Robyn Ramsay

I sit at my writing desk gazing out through the windows of my traditional home at Maleny, high in the mountains of south east Queensland, Australia. The fire is crackling nearby and the garden is fresh and green from a recent downpour. Our beloved family dog is curled up asleep beside me, my first book has recently been published, and my new grandson has visited with his family. The future is promising with new writing projects and travel opportunities with my partner. A settled feeling that comes with finding a nourishing community to live in falls upon me. And I reflect upon the words staring at me from the desk calendar:

"Wellbeing is lined up outside your door. Everything you have ever desired, whether spoken or unspoken, has been transmitted by you vibrationally. It has been heard and understood by Source and has been answered. Now you are going to allow yourself to receive it."

My reality in the early 90's however, looked very different to this quote from the book *Ask and it is Given*, by Jerry and Esther Hicks. Recently separated from a twenty-year marriage, I had two young daughters to raise and little prospect of finding well-paid work in our seaside tourist town. Emotions, mainly based around the fear of being alone, were still very raw and painful. The prospect of moving to a city to re-establish myself elsewhere was a daunting prospect. Good friends, a supportive local school community, and our comfortable home highset among the trees, were three reasons why I chose to stay despite looming financial issues.

I had always been an enterprising person and fortunate with career opportunities, co-writing and directing a significant film in London called *Go For It*, which explores youth unemployment. Similar schemes had followed back in Australia where I trained indigenous community health workers. Offered employment as Community Development Officer in Northern Queensland, I was given the task of establishing a new community center providing varied facilities for residents. Over the ensuing months, I set up opportunity shops for the trading of second-hand goods in the community and programs for the exchange of baby and children's equipment, vacation care, and so forth. An unstoppable force for implementing new ideas, I truly resonated with the phrase *just do it* to describe my passion for first visualizing and then creating or manifesting my ideas.

I noticed that others would question my vision, focusing on how I was going to achieve my goals rather than the desired outcome. This very focus on the *how* instead of the *what* led many people to abandon their passions. The alternative I had discovered, was to trust the "wellbeing lined up outside the door" that would bring a desired outcome into reality. I also observed the speed with which one person's positive outlook and one enthusiastic idea would then be taken up and supported by a seemingly endless supply of workers and well-wishers. The second hand stores and baby exchange programs for example were promptly flooded by clothing, toys, and equipment.

It seemed that volunteers were ready and eager to participate in such schemes, but unable to make the transition from ideas to action. Additionally, many people were unconsciously waiting for approval from some outside authority, as if to be granted permission to pursue their passion. My latter years as a counselor, illustrated time and again that many people focus on the *how* rather than *what* they would love in life. This generally followed on from deep-seated childhood beliefs and the need of parental approval. We are directly or inadvertently taught as children to be cautious and wary, to expect the worst of a situation, and that life is tough and is more about scarcity than abundance. This in turn heightens our fears about change or new challenges. Experience in my own life with following through many ideas and projects, gradually provided me with a mantra of sorts: *Just do it!*

I was to have many opportunities to put this to the test.

So there I was, recently turned forty, when the abundance and relative ease of life appeared to be ending. Separated after a lengthy marriage and with the responsibilities of rearing children, it was foreseeable that tough times lay ahead. My timber home, now on the market to sell, was riddled with termites creating alarming dust piles on the floors on a daily basis. Few job opportunities were available, and one of the low points in my life involved registering at the social security office for a single mother's pension. I had recently and unsuccessfully dated Paul, a charming man with whom I became rapidly attached. With little warning, he soon pulled away from me with no apparent reason. Hurt, inexperienced with the dating game, and wanting to question him further, I arranged that we meet for coffee. This simple meeting was to have far reaching consequences on the future direction of my life. What he told me would have a profound effect on my understanding about passion and purpose.

Concurrently, in my home town, two practitioners in the health industry approached me with a most unexpected and generous offer. They proposed that I join their lively practice, renting the third available room to develop my own allied business. Although flattered that they had specifically chosen me, my perception was that I had nothing to offer them. A trained teacher by trade, I had experienced an incredible series of fortunate career breaks in my life. A seemingly invisible force had carried me along thus far, placing one opportunity after another in position. This provided me a wealth of diverse experiences. The appealing proposal to join a thriving natural health center however, was one I simply could not accept. I had no skills to offer the practice apart from limited meditation and massage skills, and a genuine humanitarian outlook and love of helping others. Reluctantly I declined their offer, quietly astonished they had even considered me. It was during the meeting with Paul over a cup of coffee that my inner voice sharply reminded me once again of the words *just do it*.

Hearing of this seemingly impossible offer, he presented me with three powerful alternatives to viewing life, from many years of personal experience. This proved to be a priceless gift at a crucial time. The first group of people he explained never recognized life opportunities that came their way. The second group recognized a life opportunity but failed to take any action. The third group recognized an opportunity and not only took action, but deliberately placed their wholehearted energy behind it.

The third option was the one Paul had chosen throughout his life. A highly successful businessman, he had implemented many innovative ideas in the yacht charter and scuba industries. That morning he shared his simple philosophy with me. He was open, alert, and passionate about recognizing and receiving life opportunities when they came his way, despite the fear of new ventures that would have undoubtedly confronted him. Paul took the action steps needed and above all put in one hundred percent of his energy. Obstacles along the way were dealt with as they arose, and he would make adjustments and realign his vision accordingly. The focus of his energy was clearly not on the *how* but on *what* he wanted.

Listening intently to what he was telling me, the hairs on my arms stood on end as if in confirmation. I knew in that moment that my association with him was in order to hear this clear message. The reason why our brief and somewhat painful relationship had failed would never be known. This information was timely and far more important for me to receive. I had been presented with a remarkable opportunity to join a practice and to make a new start for myself. It was a career challenge that would develop in ways unseen to provide me with joy, abundance, and financial and emotional stability. Here was an opportunity, I recognized it as such and decided to take action. Turning down the street from the café, I walked to the building that housed Whitsunday Natural Health to meet with my new landlords and to accept their kind offer.

So it was that I commenced my new business within these welcoming walls, initially taking appointments for simple remedial massages and training in meditation for beginners. Subscribing to the idea *if life gives you lemons, make lemonade,* I considered taking full advantage of the endless tourist traffic through our town. There was little to do on wet days in a seaside town and I had soon developed enjoyable two-day workshops teaching the basics of massage and meditation. The selling of therapeutic products such as oils, tables, and books provided additional income and was a natural, organic flow-on from this activity. Advertising, business cards, editorial coverage, and the growing reputation gained from satisfied clients, soon led to a stream of bookings from newly arrived tourists.

During these early years I was aware that many massage sessions were thinly disguised counselling sessions for clients, where intense discussion of personal issues took place. I recognized a valuable opportunity here to expand my repertoire of services. Feeling encouraged by an expanding interest in the healing and helping industry, I enrolled in a correspondence course for counselling. Studying and creating workshops had inadvertently developed my passion for writing.

An extraordinary opening then occurred to enable me to act on this new ability. I would not have become a published writer some ten years later if I had failed to recognize another powerful opportunity that came my way.

Preparing a resort room to massage the editor of the new and inspirational *Pure Health* magazine, I was greeted by a vibrant and enthusiastic young woman. She announced that she was seeking a person in the north of Australia to join a well paid team of feature, travel, and health writers for her Sydney-based operation. I was her choice for the position. It was a stunning and inexplicable offer. And to this day I do not know how this gift came so swiftly and with such ease. Informing her that I was not a published writer, my well-practiced inner voice resonated with those words: *just do it.*

Within weeks I was on my way to Sydney for photo shoots with the editorial team. I wrote many feature articles for that magazine, the very first of which was titled *A Woman's Intuition*. I recall asking the editor why she had chosen me that day to join her crew. She coyly replied, "Just call it a woman's intuition."

The natural health center continued to thrive. Eventually taking over the lease, I expanded my therapy rooms into two local resorts and employed additional staff. Regular clients included VIPs, film celebrities, and media moguls in search of respite from their daily responsibilities. I had become a successful businesswoman in my own right. These active and productive years remain some of the happiest in my life. I followed my intuition and my passion. Extraordinary opportunities manifested, the greatest of which was my published writing. It enabled me to be generous with the needs of my growing children. After eight years, the practice sold with ease, to a woman who unexpectedly paid me a visit with an offer that was impossible to refuse. I continued to travel the world before finally purchasing a home in the mountains, where my time could be devoted to writing books.

Emotionally it was a decade of healing the wounds of relationship separation. The lessons learned during that time were to trust my intuition and wisdom, to make my own decisions, and to listen and follow my heart. Even more so, to recognize opportunities that come my way and give myself permission to take action. To this day I have remained true to, and continue to recommend to others, the simple philosophy *just do it* in regard to finding purpose and passion in life.

About the Author

Robyn Ramsay, recently published author of *Finding Duong: Finding Myself*, is an inspirational presenter and a celebrant. Her life combines years of socially conscious travel and multicultural experiences with counselling and different modalities in the healing profession. She trained in social artistry leadership with Dr. Jean Houston from the UN and Magicians Way with William Whitecloud. Robyn has studied in depth, the work of Joseph Campbell, Robert Fritz, and Peter Senge, world leaders in the exploration of profound change in people, organizations, and society. Robyn is devoted in her writing and speaking engagements, to assisting people to connect more deeply with one another and with their common concerns and sense of purpose.

She lives in Maleny Australia with partner, Gary, and Wups the dog, writing aboard the family canal boat for several months each year in France.

http://www.robynramsay.com

A HOME FROM MY HEART

Alana Peake

In April 2001, I was a shy, artistic girl just getting by at school. I loved to learn, but did *not* enjoy being there. I was fortunate to have a group of good friends who made school life more than bearable. However, outside this group I felt very anxious. I would not go into a store alone because I was too shy to look the shop assistant in the eye. I had a low self-image, no confidence, and often felt powerless, as if I could not do anything right. At home I barely came out of my room. I was always reading, drawing, and writing stories, songs, or poetry, which reflected my rather depressed emotional state.

It was my last year of high school and one autumn day, after an afternoon class was cancelled, I walked in the sun to the public library to research an assignment on animal biology. It was an easy assignment and as soon as I finished, I rewarded myself by pursuing my own interests in the New Age section. I was deeply fascinated with dream interpretation and palmistry, and I indulged myself by delving into this subject for the rest of the day.

After some serious hours of browsing, I went back to the shelves in search of something different; something I knew nothing about; something I could take home with me. As I scanned the books, I noticed a little white book standing out amongst the larger ones. It seemed to leap out at me whispering, "Choose me! Read Me!"

After reading the book's blurb, I was intrigued by the term *Divine Substance*. The book spoke of creating what you wanted in your life through manifestation and, having never heard of the concept before, I was fascinated by it. This was a book I was eager to get home and start reading. What I learned in that book changed my life.

The book emphasized, as a starting point to bringing your desires to life, that it is imperative to put them on paper. And so I purchased a small floral note book, thought about what I wanted, and wrote very neatly the things I wanted to manifest. Of the five things I wrote, there was one that I felt absolutely passionate about: owning our own family-home. Although we had been securely housed in a beautiful long-term leased home in an upmarket area surrounded by lagoons and shady trees, I worried a lot about renting. I knew rent would go up in the years to come because where we lived was not only a tourist hot spot close to the World Heritage listed Fraser Island, but also one of the fastest growing regional cities in Australia. My family – (Mum, Dad and little brother Kyle) – was my world and I wanted us to have a home base and security in the future.

So I wrote, "I want my family to have their own wonderful home by the year 2005," and at the bottom of the page, "This or something better, Father. Let the Divine result now appear." On the front cover of the little notebook I wrote, "May all in this book be for the good of all and to the detriment of none." I then closed the book and put it on my desk amongst the general clutter of a teenager's life.

And I forgot all about it.

Three months passed before my parents received a call from the landlord. His wife had been hospitalized and, though she was fine, her health-scare had resulted in her wanting to live in her own dream home: our rental house. After almost four years of stability, we had two months to find somewhere else. This was a very insecure and worrying time for my family because there were few rentals available at the time, most of them unsuitable. And when they were suitable we were competing with many other equally desperate people.

The weeks were passing and we had no place to go. In a very emotional moment my dad expressed how much he hated moving and vowed that he would do everything possible never to be in this position again. "We will just have to buy our own place," he said.

This was astonishing because in my whole lifetime I had never heard my parents even considering this option. I was very excited and went straight to my desk, dug out the notebook and thought, "Wow! It's happening!"

Just two weeks before we had to vacate, feeling insecure and worried about the future, a short-term rental became available. It was in a perfect location, literally just around the corner from where we were living. We applied for the lease and were accepted, and over the next couple of weeks (with little expense and many trips) we gradually moved into what would be our very last rental, because from then on my parents began to seriously look at properties for sale.

One day they stopped off to visit a friend of the family and he mentioned that the vacant block next door was up for sale. It was a big bush block, with a great neighbor, and as my dad worked in the next town not far from this land, it meant he would travel less distance and have more time for family life. *How convenient!* It was a little expensive but we could make an offer. It seemed that everything was in line with my desires and things were falling into place better than I could have hoped.

So an offer was made on my 18th birthday and was *rejected*. I was so upset and worried that we weren't going to get the land which we were all, by then, so excited about. I constantly and obsessively thought, "We have to get it! We just have to."

Finally, after a miserable week of indecision and worried contemplation looking at options, my family made the decision to pay the listed price.

Within a week we were land owners.

Then it was full steam ahead. Trucks and machinery were bought in to clear parts of the land. There were the normal hassles with builders' schedules and materials not arriving on time. There were challenges for us with deadlines that had to be met, but life was changing and becoming more exciting. In time, the house was erected and Mum and Dad worked to meet the contract deadlines, doing all the interior fixtures to save on the building costs.

This was a time when the whole family worked together. When I got home from school, Mum and my brother would be preparing to go out to the house site, and as soon as Dad got home from work they would be off. With Mum, Dad, and my brother gone, I would do my part by becoming chief cook and bottle washer, and by preparing dinner for the family. And despite being hardly ever in my room anymore, I felt involved and useful and I loved it!

By November we were all working to get the house finished. My dad's sister, my favorite and only aunty, came from Hawaii to visit and help with my high school graduation and prom. Christmas came and went and in the New Year I enrolled in college. Then, on the 11th of March 2002 it happened: we moved into our new home.

That was such a surreal experience.

Looking back years later I see that not everything on my list came true but the one thing I wanted with a passion – for my family to have their own home – did come true and in record time. I realize there needs to be a burning desire to fuel the manifestation, not merely just a vague wish. When that passionate desire was present it only took three months to begin manifesting and we were in our own home in less than a year.

I had found that library book at age seventeen when I had next to no self-confidence. When I wrote my desire for a family-home I had no idea how that desire could become a reality. I didn't really believe it was possible. All I had was a dream and a passionate desire for the greater good of my family.

This showed me that knowing what you want and why you want it is very important: if you know the *what* and the *why*, the *how* will look after itself.

I never imagined exactly what I wanted the house to look like. I simply wanted us to have a house of our own. I now feel my original desire was the catalyst for the Universe to tap into each of us and deliver exactly what we wanted: A home on acreage where my brother could ride his motor bike, where Dad could build a shed and work from home, where Mum could organize and design a garden, and where I could find peace of mind and security for my family together.

Remember the little floral notebook and the front cover where I wrote, "May all in this book be for the good of all and to the detriment of none"? Well there was a very positive flow-on-effect from that affirmation. Our old landlord and his wife are very happy to be in their dream home. The temporary accommodation we lived in prior to moving into our own house is now the home of my aunty who fell in love with it.

I now know we *can* change our futures. Being honest with yourself about what you want for you and your life is vital and is a lesson I continue to learn. Sometimes we can get caught up in what other people want for us and lose sight of who we are, what we want, and where we are going. Denial is like a second nature to many of us, but as soon as you put it aside and are completely honest with yourself, you will find your passion.

Write this passion down and the path will be made clear.

I have continued to manifest amazing things in my life. From my career to my relationships of love and friendship, I have had an abundance of experiences which I am eternally grateful for. I now know that when I say out loud I passionately want something, and keep that passionate thought in my mind for days, then that very thing will come into existence.

Not long ago a good friend asked me what my passion was. What was I passionate about in terms of my career? I knew I wanted to do something creative and expressive, but never had a clear answer for him. The last time he asked, I burst into tears and said in a vulnerable but powerful voice, "I want to write!"

He asked me, "What do you want to write?"

I replied, "I don't know... I just want to write something!"

I felt amazingly good after expressing my desire as if I had been freed from a very small and restrictive cage. I had been denying what I really wanted for so long. Just two weeks later I applied to be an author in the *Adventures in Manifesting* series and here I am. I am writing!

I now believe we are all here for a purpose. Each one of us has so much potential and can do amazing things. We can create miracles in our lives and in the lives of others' as well. So this is my hope for all: Let your hearts voice be heard and watch your life unfold like the beautiful flower it is and was always meant to be.

Light and love to all.

About the Author

Alana Peake is an aspiring writer, dedicated Reiki practitioner, and multi-talented creative artist with an appreciation of nature. She has a special bond with animals and birds, and shares her home with four beautiful cockatiels and a cheeky quaker parrot named Spud (who seems to know more than he lets on).

Fascinated by the metaphysical, she loves all things creative and inspirational and believes passionately in the healing power of truth, love, and creativity. She holds a diploma of visual arts, is currently studying for a degree in psychology, and hopes to have an art therapy practice in the future.

Alana relishes in the company of those she loves but also enjoys solitude. She is an empathic and loves to make friends and create joy wherever she goes. Alana believes we all have an inner light and it is up to each one of us how brightly we shine.

http://www.alanapeake.com

WHO ARE YOU, REALLY?

Terry L. Newbegin

Have you ever asked yourself why you may not be receiving your share of miracles? Do you often think that it might be tied to your human identity, where you were born, your education level, or possibly a lack of faith in God, making you feel unworthy of His love and miracles?

Do you often feel lost, depressed, and neglected and attribute it to the world economy, our politicians, or terrorists? When witnessing brutal storms that don't show mercy for anyone, including the poor, or physically and mentally challenged, do you lose faith in life?

Don't give up on life just yet – for you hold more power than you think. You see, it is not about God's level of love for you or anyone else. It is about how *passionate* you are in knowing who you truly are.

I have had my share of failures in life and much confusion about God, His miracles, and His teachings. I have even felt alone and unworthy of His love. I know that you might feel trapped and don't know what to do, where to go, or who to turn to; however, you probably may never have thought about your human identity as being less than three percent of all that you are.

If you are experiencing little to no miracles in your life, and feel that all you experience is disappointment, it could be because the eminence of all that you are is missing.

What is your eminence? It is your soul!

Yes, your soul is the real Christ waiting for you to become awakened to it. Believe me. Your soul knows who you are, where (and who) you have been, and the types of things that are important to you.

Your soul knows *everything* about you.

My dear friends, it takes a brave person to stop, take a deep breath, and *listen* to their soul, because the mind is programmed for rejection. It is trained to justify everything by blaming circumstances and others for all suffering. When you can learn to *observe* what is taking place in your mind, you shall begin to identify with the importance of who you truly are and what your life purpose is.

Some religions maintain that the Bible spells it out unequivocally that you suffer due to sin. I'm here to tell you that what you are experiencing in the present has *nothing* to do with sin, the end of the world, or about Jesus returning to collect those that feel blameless. What is misunderstood is how religions and governments have made everything complex and mystifying when it comes to God, Satan, your soul, your intellect, and how you should be managed.

And, the best way to keep everything managed is to have you obsessed with fear, punishment, guilt, and patriotism.

By keeping you locked into the conventional belief about God, sin, and you being only human, those in authority preserve their power in setting up the ground rules to control your beliefs; thus, manipulating what you experience as your reality. With the conditioning of the mind through religion, education, and government, the probability of you experiencing anxiety, uncertainty, drama, despair, depression, and lack of miracles increases to nearly one hundred percent. This is because of the way you measure yourself as a human.

To step into the consciousness of mastering your own life, you must understand *who you truly are.* You must realize that you give up free choice when you tie it to your beliefs and to your allegiance to family, church, and government. Hence, you give up on the fact that *you are in control of your own life purpose.*

For instance, I was born and raised in a tiny house that managed to squeeze in seven people. I believed that I was poor, uneducated, and only human, thereby being preconditioned to failure.

Once I graduated from high school, I continued to live in my preconditioned reality. I lived this way for several years before I began to believe that I could make it as an entrepreneur. Of course, my first question was, "Where am I going to get money to launch a business?"

My family had no money, and I knew no one that would loan it to me.

Nevertheless, even though I was young and naive, and believed I was destined to being poor and uneducated... that did not stop me. I may have lacked the skills and financial status to start a business in comparison to someone who was born into money and was college-educated. It all boiled down to believing in myself more than what type of environment I was born into, whether I had a college business degree and access to money, or not.

It was the year 1971. I was in my early twenties when money finally found me by providing me with not one, but three partners. Since I was the one with the experience in this start-up business, I became the president of the company.

The business lasted three and a half years before going bankrupt in 1975. This unfortunately led to my personal bankruptcy, as well. This situation was very devastating, to say the least, but my passion to be in business prevailed.

Eight months later, in December of 1975, I went back into business. This time, I had one partner. My business adventure lasted from 1975 to 1993 before my world, once again, was turned upside down when I was thrown out of my own company. It was a time in my life when I believed God and my education of high school years had forsaken me. It truly hurt deep within my soul. At first, my thoughts went to God and how I threw Him out of my life at a very young age, which justified to me God's lack of miracles in my life.

In the spring of 1993, I actually began to fear God on a level of so much anxiety and dismay that I thought I was doomed for the rest of my life. I had lost my passion for becoming an entrepreneur, and I had succumbed to my destiny of failure. I even had thoughts about attending church again, wondering if maybe I could *save myself* from God's wrath.

Although I was thinking and feeling this way deeply, something was still eating at me. Intuitively I began to feel that my failures had nothing to do with my former partners, my education level, my belief in God, or where I was born.

There was obviously something greater to it than this.

Following several months of prayer and of feeling depressed, betrayed, as well as allowing my mind to put me down, I could not take these feelings anymore. So, I slowly began to take deep breaths. At first, it was only for a few minutes a day, and then I worked up to thirty minutes a day.

While I was doing this deep breathing, unconsciously knowing of its later effects, for several months I felt my mind put me down as a failure before I began to notice that it was beginning to slow down as far as downcasting me. Even my thoughts of depression and betrayal began to decelerate. It was a time in my life that I really felt my emotions on a conscious level and how out of balance I had become.

Yes, failing twice in business and losing my income hurt. Not only because I felt betrayed by someone whom I thought was my friend, but I felt clumsy, foolish, stupid, frustrated, and, worst yet, I believed that I let my family down. Instead of trying to remain positive and force those feelings out of my mind, I allowed those emotional feelings to *come into* my heart.

I said to myself, "It hurts but my family and I are okay; worried, but okay.

Then one day, while I was sitting alone doing my deep breathing exercises in silence, I began to sense someone speaking to me. When I first felt this vibrational forum, I thought that maybe my mind had fallen into the mode of making things up. Yet, in spite of what my mind was judging it to be, the feeling was just too overwhelming for me to ignore.

This is when I realized it was something higher than me that was speaking.

Somehow, I just knew within my entire being that this was not something coming from my mind or from anyone else, physically or ethereally.

It was coming from my soul.

This is what my soul conveyed to me:

"I am you at a higher level – for I am your soul and I have come forward to help you learn who you truly are. I am here at this time for your awakening and to reveal to you the true nature of miracles, and the why of it all being a mystery to you. It is not about your business, education, where you were born, your intellect, your intelligence, your failures, or about God. It is about

the wisdom that you have learned from every experience and encounter that you have had with yourself, with your past lifetimes, and with others."

It was then that I decided to let God and all ties to religion go and to trust only what I was intuitively feeling from my soul. Once I let go, including what the government and my church wanted me to believe in, I felt my soul supporting me.

Before I knew it, my soul again conveyed to me its wisdom:

"Your path of many lifetimes contains the wisdom of your experiences. When you place all that you are only in this lifetime, because of your beliefs and who you think you are as a human, then I, your soul, cannot bring forth the wisdom of those experiences to you. Because of this, you and I have been separated. For being aware of who you truly are as also a Christ is more important than all the treasures of the world."

It was from my deep breathing exercises that I had finally connected to my soul: the Christ within me. My soul did not care about my intelligence, money, success, fame, or what I thought about God, my church, or my government. All that my soul wanted was for me to become aware of who I truly am: *a divine being.* Once I understood this, miracles of abundance, healing, and joy came to me effortlessly.

It was now that I decided to open up another business for the third time and become a competitor to my former partner. In September of 1993, I incorporated my new company and worked out of my home until spring of 1994.

From April to December of 1994, my sales were about $94,000. This allowed me to move into a leased building. Today, in the year 2012, my annual sales are in the millions. I have written two books, with a third coming out soon, and here I am co-authoring with other well-known authors in this book.

If you believe in destiny, that you are only human, a sinner, or that you have to attend church to be worthy of miracles, then you are processing who you are in an intellectual way and not through your soul. Intellectual energy coming from the mind will always teach you that you must make a choice according to who you believe you are, what you have been taught by the masses, and what characterizes you as a human.

From the time I was born to my mid-fifties, I learned the hard way before I found the secret behind God's miracles.

True miracles don't come from God or from anyone else; they come from you. Your soul is Christ in disguise.

Stop and look at your life situations. Observe why you may be struggling through life. Sit in a relaxed place of silence, do deep breathing exercises, and allow your soul to come in and join you. Your soul will show you the patterns of your dogmatic beliefs and how you have been blindly following them due to fear and cultural tradition.

When you learn to move beyond your mind's structured and conditioned beliefs, your soul's essence will make its appearance. Your soul will not care if you are a king, a queen, a president of a country, a drunk, a drug addict, or a non-believer in God.

All your soul wants is to join you and show you how divine you are.

It wants to combine your mind, body, and soul into one unit. Once you have reached this place, you can live passionately and with purpose.

About the Author

Terry L. Newbegin of Johnson City, Tennessee, was born in Caribou, Maine, in 1948. He married in 1967 and has four children whom are now grown and have blessed Terry with loving grandchildren.

Terry has written three books, *Genesis: Your Journey Home (2nd Edition)*, *The Book of Revelation: A New Beginning*, and *Unlocking the Consciousness of Your Soul*, which is due out this Fall.

Although Terry has been a successful entrepreneur for over thirty years, his greatest passion is to bring in new energy consciousness that extends beyond the traditional vibrational energy of the Bible. He is an innovative prophet, and a pioneer in new energy at a time when religious beliefs are all based on conventional understanding.

Terry has a lifelong history of having an open mind, heart, and call for consciousness awakening.

http://www.terrynewbegin.com

TO DREAM, BELIEVE, CREATE, AND SUCCEED

Amber Walker

Occasionally, feeling lonely and sad is normal. Feeling as though life is so bad that you want to kill yourself, is not.

At twenty-two years of age it was hard to fathom why I hated myself so much and why I felt so worthless, useless, and lonely. I had previously been diagnosed and hospitalized with depression when I was just eighteen. However this time around was worse. Much worse. Physical pain literally radiated through my body. I hit rock bottom and was convinced life was so painful that it had to end.

At the time I was studying at university, trying to get out of a fitness career that I thought was taking me nowhere. I worked in modelling and promotions, hospitality, and even dabbled in real-estate to pay the bills. Most people would say I was a happy and bubbly person, but what people saw and perceived was but a façade. In fact, I had been so depressed for so long that I learnt to hide it, pretending I was happy and fulfilled. On the inside however, I was crumbling, broken, and exhausted.

Eventually this masquerade of being a happy person tumbled down. I just couldn't pretend anymore.

It all started in the emergency ward. There, I was told I could either go home or get help. It was apparent I needed help so I agreed on being transferred to a private hospital in Eastern Melbourne, where the hospital's top psychiatrist assessed me. With my family's long history of depression, and a range of nasty events occurring during my late teenage years, I was at last happy to speak with a professional that would finally be able to help my condition. This happiness was short-lived.

When the psychiatrist intensely frowned and told me I was a very difficult case and that he was incapable of helping, I was horrified. He said that he would however keep seeing me until someone else would take me on.

"What? A very difficult case? Incapable of helping me?" I thought. The feelings of disappointment, when all I craved was stability and compassion, were overwhelming.

I felt annoyed and frustrated that the very people in this hospital were meant to be the best in their field. And then I get told that I'm a difficult case and that they can't help me? If they couldn't help me, I would have next to no hope that anyone could. Looking back in my diary, this is a time in my life when I began to lose the sense, or at best, the value of time. I lost not only days, but weeks. In my diary I wrote nothing. However I do remember staring at walls, pulling hair out of my head, and crying for several days back-to-back trying to figure out why nobody could help me.

A common theme exposed itself: events in my life had led me to feel a certain way; to feel neglected, alone, and disappointed. The events were all different yet the feelings were all the same. Once again, I was relying and depending on others to make me feel better when, in fact, other people no matter how highly qualified they were, weren't capable of supplying me with the feelings I needed.

It was going to be up to me to find those positive feelings for myself.

I began to look at my life and realized I merely existed; life was a chore; I had no dreams, desires or passions. I was trying to fit into a society by being ordinary, rather than seeking for something extraordinary. When I brought this up with my psychiatrist, he suggested I settle down, adjust to a mundane daily routine, and not disappoint myself by striving for too much. This was the very person who had stated he couldn't help me! But he was wrong.

I had already decided I was going to find these feelings for myself. Saying it wouldn't help to find a consuming passion that'd allow me to do something extraordinary was just extra motivation for me. It set my wheels in motion to find a way to make it work, and to prove the doctor wrong.

In the hospital there was a quote that hung on the wall. It read, "Dream, Believe, Create, Succeed." I immediately wrote the quote in my diary. If I was to feel positive, I had to start surrounding myself with positive energy. I started collecting quotes each day, from spiritual leaders to sportspeople and politicians. The quotes were very inspirational and made me think of what my life could be. For the first time of my adult life I began to envisage a happy future. At the end of each day, I would come back to that one quote: "Dream, Believe, Create, Succeed."

If I broke it down, this was something I could live by. First, I needed a dream. Second, I had to believe in the dream. And finally, I had to put the steps into action to make the dream possible; when all of this was done, I would succeed and reap the rewards.

My first dream was simple: to be happy with myself.

Despite having absolutely *no* idea what that meant, I started to believe I did have the right to be happy, and that settling for an ordinary nine-to-five job, because some doctor told me so, was just not going to cut it. When I was finally able to leave the hospital after six weeks I took the plunge, leaving my studies and jobs to visit a friend in the tropical city of Darwin. I was not completely reckless; at first this was just a holiday and I had planned on returning. Yet upon returning I truly began to believe in my dream and knew that aiming for a stable job in Melbourne was not going to make me happy. I left most of my belongings, packed up a suitcase, and headed to Darwin. I decided I would start working in a bar until I discovered my passion. I still didn't realize what it was but knew that I had to find it and still truly believed that it was there.

Shortly after arriving in Darwin, I once again had time for fitness and reconnected with it as a way to ease the pain of my depression. Although I had come out of my deep gloomy state, I was still vulnerable and knew I had to continuously push myself to find the motivation to succeed in my quest.

In Darwin I found a partner who was perfect for me at the time. Though it might sound harsh, he was the perfect partner because he was not around for me to rely on. Working offshore on his fishing vessel meant I had to rely on myself for motivation and the desire to live. I knew I was not in a mental state to become dependent on someone else. When I became pregnant my friends and family were more than concerned, believing that I would now revert to my old ways and relapse into another depressive episode. Throughout my pregnancy I kept active and maintained my diary of positive quotes.

After giving birth to my first child, I began to feel myself relapse and began to feel trapped. Once again I realized I was relying on others to give me positive feelings rather than finding and creating them for myself. I focused on my daughter but knew this was a temporary fix; that to be successful and a good mother I had to focus on myself.

After my second child, I began to feel a real desire to pursue a passion for myself. With my love of fitness, I decided a competitive sport would be the ideal activity for me to focus on. With a husband that worked at sea, sometimes for months at a time, a full-time job in television sales, and with no out-of-work-hours daycare in gyms, I decided that body sculpting was a sport I could train for at home. I did not have a full gym set up, but being a personal trainer for over ten years allowed me to improvize and train with the children after work and on the weekends.

I had found my passion.

At the beginning of my journey, I decided to write down my goals and visualize what it was I wanted to achieve. I decided I wanted to be one of the top five body sculptors in the world within five years. When I told my family and friends, the response was one of laughter and questioning as to *why* I would want to do such a thing. My response was that I wanted to have a passion; that I needed something extraordinary to strive for; that I didn't want to merely exist when I could really be living.

I went about training in the park, much to the amusement of the other mothers. I used household chores as exercise routines and danced to children's DVDs for extra cardio. I was strict with my diet and even began encouraging some of the other Mothers in the park to join in.

I did all this not only whilst having a full-time job and looking after two toddlers on my own, but also while running my husbands business and managing his bookwork at night.

Then there were the people. They started to say I was crazy and that I would never have the time. Little did they know I *chose* to make the time. I was passionate about something for the first time of my adult life and it felt amazing. It was at this time that my belief astronomically grew and I began to foresee my future in the health and fitness industry. I would write for hours in my diary about the sponsorships I hoped to attract and the website (that would aim at empowering women) I wanted to build. I truly began writing my destiny and watched as what I had written unfolded.

When I won my first competition I still had a lot of work to do, so I went about my playground workouts with my head down and my bottom up. It came as a surprise when I won the Asia Pacific Best Body title, but what came as more of a shock was winning the World Best Body Championship in New York City three weeks later. My dream had come true and I had achieved my goal of being in the World's top five body sculptors within five years.

It was only the week before I left Australia that I wrote in my diary about how I would look and feel on stage in New York. I wrote exactly what I would look like holding the World Championship trophy, from the shape of my body to the color of my tan. I truly believed that against the odds of being just five months into the sport and with two young toddlers, it was possible to win a World Best Body Championship. Just as I had manifested, this World Championship title led to sponsorships, the development of my website, and a second World Championship title a year later.

Though my early years were tough and I had come from a dark place, I believe this experience was necessary to bring me to where I am today, allowing me to understand that there are times when everything is not perfect but that you can use the power of manifestation to entirely change your life. My focus and passion has now shifted to motivating and inspiring other women to live not only a healthy and active life, but to also live their dreams.

Remember nothing is too extreme and nothing is too small. Search for your own passion. When you have control of your own feelings you can begin seizing opportunities and living the purposeful life you have always dreamed of.

About the Author

Amber Walker is a three time WNBF (World Natural Bodybuilding Federation) world's best-body championship winner, personal trainer, fitness writer, TV presenter and motivational speaker. Amber is also a proud mother of two children.

With a strong athletic background in sports ranging from gymnastics to track and field, teamed with education in bio-medical science and personal training Amber uses her knowledge and experience to educate, motivate and inspire others to live a healthy and active life. Her passion is to help women and mothers reach for their dreams. By setting yourself challenges she believes you can really take control of your own destiny and that there is no greater waste in life than wondering what could have been.

http://www.amberwalker.com

RADIATING LOVE AND JOY

Anne McClure Deatly

Until two years ago, the hectic pace of my stressful life led to my health's deterioration, an unbalanced lifestyle, misplaced priorities, and a total disconnection from my authentic self. I was overwhelmed, raising two children alone, and struggling to meet demanding deadlines of a research scientist.

It was an ego-generated race. Scientific discoveries and the number of publications dictated my identity in the world. I focused on *doing* rather than *being*, leaving me wondering: *is this it?*

Opening myself to new possibilities was a choice that radically improved my life.

My life reflected my strong faith. I attended worship regularly on Sunday mornings and Wednesday evenings, and was very involved with church activities; serving as an elder, and teaching Sunday school and adult education classes. I chaired committees such as missions and social concerns and children's ministries. But I was operating from a mental-based program. My heart was not the key force leading my actions. I meditated and was connected to the divine... but not deeply enough.

A friend recommended a set of CDs by Eckhart Tolle entitled, *Stillness Speaks*. I listened to them almost a hundred times during my trips to and from work. Something very powerful shifted within me. Perhaps new neural pathways developed in my brain or existing pathways were re-wired. Perhaps there was an energy shift at the cellular level. Regardless, there definitely was an awakening of my inner spirit.

My highest potential simply could not be reached on my previous path, for it didn't reflect the essence of my authentic nature. Eckhart Tolle emphasized the importance of surrendering the ego, which was another factor inhibiting my true nature. Changing my life path would require surrendering the outcome of my actions and living in flow. Spending quality time in silence and stillness would allow inspirations and my essence to come through me without resistance. My heart, rather than my ego, would lead my life.

This very shift was the beginning of a journey of transformation and living authentically. As a principal research scientist, I studied viruses and bacteria to make new vaccines. When my children entered adulthood and started living independently, I had tremendous freedom. I could go anywhere and... do anything! Intellectually, it made sense that my new path would lead me to transfer vaccine research technology to scientists in developing countries.

After weeks of searching the internet, no opportunity presented itself. Not one. Nothing was available with the United Nations, Save the Children, the Bill and Melinda Gates Foundation. Nothing. Most jobs listed were administrative jobs. No scientific opportunities were available for someone with my credentials. And like a thunderbolt from heaven, it struck me that I was trying to force something to happen! This obviously wasn't my new path. I *surrendered* knowing an inspiration would come at the appropriate time to follow a new path.

Months later, I started hearing about energy medicine. With nine different energy systems, the body has the capability of healing itself. Energy medicine is the practice of balancing energies for vibrancy and harmony. To learn more, I ordered an energy medicine kit and received it just days before a weekend workshop in New York City, a few miles from my home.

Realizing the significance of this timing, a powerful energetic shift shook me from deep within and, acting on this inspiration, I attended the workshop. My heart soared learning there was a two-year certification program starting in less than two weeks! My hopes and excitement however were disenchanted when I heard attendance at a five-day program was required for registration.

Disappointed, I dismissed the idea of starting the program that year.

For the following several days, however, an internal force nudged me to investigate how to overcome the prerequisite hurdle, and so I called the company, Innersource. My heart was ecstatic to learn a five-day program DVD set was available and I agreed to take a test. In a matter of minutes, I had bought the DVD set, registered for the certification program, and gotten a plane ticket. This was my introductory experience to living in flow with the Universe.

From knowledge gained in the first class, I incorporated the daily energy routine of simple exercises to obtain and maintain balanced harmony of my energy systems. Energetic changes were cumulative. My energy systems adjusted to new patterns of flow after only months of exercising. My energy levels were higher, my vibration was higher, and my body was at peace.

No longer was I resisting life; I was living in flow with it. If a stressful situation arose, I could hold my main neurovascular points and prevent the stress response. Living in this revitalized and rejuvenated energetic state empowered me to take risks and be open to even more changes in my life. As I embraced the principles of energy medicine, my life evolved naturally into a new way of feeling, thinking, and living.

My life's journey had taken a new turn. Transforming my energies facilitated a further life transformation and energy medicine became my passion and purpose. Learning energy medicine taught me how valuable staying on purpose and living my passion was to my health.

But I discovered yet an even deeper passion and purpose quite unexpectedly.

I was listening to The Wellness Revolution with Adoley Odunton of Inspired Living. She was talking to Dr. Alex Loyd, author of The Healing Codes. According to Dr. Loyd, who has asked over 20,000 people what they really want in life, 99% of the general public does not know. Stunned and elated, was I one of the lucky 1% who knew their life's purpose?

Dr. Loyd inspired the audience to answer three questions honestly without filtering. He asked us to write down the first answer that arose from our guts or hearts, and invited us to release any limitations blocking us from the infinite possibilities of this discernment.

The three questions were:

1. What do you really want in life, right now this minute?

2. How would this benefit you? What would change in your life if you got want you want?

3. How would this make you feel?

According to Dr. Loyd, the answer to the third question reflects what a person really wants. Most people respond to the first question with something external. It is usually related to health, wealth, relationships, or career. The answer to the third question is usually something internal. The answer to *how would that make you feel* is usually an inner feeling or inner state of being.

Most people believe they need the external to get to the internal state. Universal principles of nature postulate otherwise: once you feel joyful or peaceful, you naturally attract health, wealth, positive relationships, and career into your life. It is the inner that produces the outer. It doesn't work the other way around.

I don't remember my answers to questions one and two. But my answer to question three changed my life values. Permanently. My answer to number three was *love and joy*. That was an awakening for me! My passion and purpose was not only to feel love and joy but also to radiate both.

Before this simple test, I wasn't conscious of this passion, but my energies strongly resonated with it. *Love and joy* are the most powerful forces in the Universe. My inner state was in alignment with Universal abundance and the connection to my higher spirit deepened.

When my energies became balanced and in harmony, I naturally felt joyful. My life got easier; I am now creating the life of my dreams.

The key to creating a life of your dreams is not only to know your true passion and purpose, but also to surrender the outcome of all your actions and be open to miracles. From childhood, we learn to judge whether something is *good* or *bad*. Life events interpreted as *bad* at the time may actually turn out to be incredible blessings and extraordinary opportunities for personal growth. Everything happens for the greater good. Challenges represent learning opportunities; chances to grow and develop in new ways. If you don't look for them, you won't find them.

What you think about… expands!

With this conscious awareness, start finding the seeds for personal growth and development. Finding seeds of opportunities make the difference between an ordinary and an extraordinary life.

To follow my passion and purpose of radiating love and joy to the world, I took a quantum leap and retired early from my scientific career. Inspired to make this quantum leap, I took the required action. I had no fear. Guided and directed, I left a good job with a steady paycheck to establish my own company: *Optimal Health and Wellness Center, LLC*, which focuses on balancing people's energy systems, teaching energy medicine, and producing health and wholeness programs. I am also in the process of becoming an inspirational speaker to spread my message about radiating love and joy.

An amazing force is creating one opportunity after another to help me spread my message of living radiantly. Amazing things naturally flow into my life now. For example, an executive producer from VoiceAmerica, the largest internet-based radio station, offered me the opportunity to be a radio talk show host for their *Health and Wellness* channel. After the initial shock, I accepted the offer and planned a thirteen-week pilot program entitled, *Energy Medicine and Optimal Health*. After eight or nine episodes, the program had a listenership of over 20,000!

VoiceAmerica offered me a new contract to continue the momentum of broadcasting my message for a year. What is most exciting is connecting to people through energetic balancing as a tool to sharing love and joy. I've become the radiant energy doctor, with the message, *Live radiantly!* The message of my show is how optimal health and energetic balance can lead to a life filled with so much love and joy that you naturally radiate that to others.

Another manifestation was selection into the Escape Velocity 212 Master Mind. As open-minded, free thinking individuals, this group will brainstorm new ways for me to share my message and inspire people to discern their passion and purpose and create the life of their dreams.

In developing myself as an inspirational speaker, I sent a short video to the Messenger Network for inclusion at the Messenger Summit in March 2012. The day the video was due I hadn't decided what to share as my message of change for the world. So I meditated and received inspiration: "Live radiantly! Radiate love and joy to the world to raise the vibration and uplift the conscious awareness."

As I prepared and sent the video, I surrendered and let go of its selection. Whatever happens is for the greater good. If this message is needed, then my video would be selected. And indeed, the video was selected along with videos from 99 other messengers. Each message is available on a website called Ripple of Change. Similar to TED Talks, this site shares only messages of change for the world. Committed to a professional speaking career, I want to transform people's lives with my story.

With divine guidance, I am living each day sharing love and joy with enthusiasm. Wonderful new opportunities are headed my way for teaching people how to create vibrant health and empowered lives. My ultimate message to you is *live radiantly!* Love and joy are the most powerful forces in the Universe. My commitment to the world is to live my life walking humbly with God sharing love and joy wherever I go.

You too can open up to new opportunities and create your dream life living your passion and purpose. Surrender and pay attention to inspirations and internal nudges. Follow the new illuminated path reflecting who you are and what you really want. Your life will become extraordinary.

About the Author

Anne M. Deatly, PhD, previously a principal research scientist in vaccine research at Pfizer, changed careers in 2012. She is now a certified Eden energy medicine practitioner, teacher, and inspirational speaker. As director of the *Optimal Health and Wellness Center,* she focuses on holistic health and energy balancing, positive inspiration, and spiritual coaching.

Energy medicine, the future of medicine, activates the body's natural healing and energy balancing system to facilitate renewal and transformation of body, mind, and spirit. Programs are designed to provide new opportunities for growth and personal development, healthy lifestyle, positive mental attitude, increased success potential, a life filled with joy, peace and harmony.

Known as the Radiant Energy Doctor, Anne is a radio talk show host *of Energy Medicine and Optimal Health* on VoiceAmerica's Health and Wellness channel. Anne was selected as one of the original messengers at the Messenger Summit in San Diego, March 2012.

http://www.radiantenergydoctor.com

DISCOVERING MY DESTINY

Cate McDonald

When it was suggested I contribute to this book, I said to myself, "Who? Me?" Then I realized I had manifested an opportunity to express my true essence and to inspire others to do the same. Why is this important to me? To answer that question, I will tell you a story of how I shifted from feeling completely invisible and with no sense of purpose to stepping into the light and discovering my destiny.

The Invisible Me

Since childhood, I've struggled with the belief that I don't matter and no-one notices the real me. I grew up in a country town where men were men and women were told who they should be. Who were these people of authority to make life-changing decisions on behalf of women who had little say in their own lives? I felt I had been born in the wrong era and I must have known, even before I arrived, that it wasn't going to be easy.

I delayed my own birth by three weeks and waited eighteen months before deciding to walk. It was already becoming clear to my mother that I wanted to be different and to not play by the rules. She said I was a shy, quiet, yet determined, little girl who did things in her own way and time, and she was right!

I began to realize that I didn't have a voice and that what I wanted wasn't important. If I was a good girl, I received love and attention; otherwise I was scolded and criticized. The authority of the church and my parents were not to be challenged. It was confusing for a little girl who just wanted to be heard and I soon became an expert at playing small so that I fitted in. I must say at this point that I had wonderful loving parents who gave me everything. I know now it was the spin I chose to put on this experience, and many others like it in my early life, which formed the belief *I don't matter.*

More about that later.

As I grew up, I felt increasingly invisible, to the extent that I believed people did not physically see me let alone notice me. This feeling was so strong and real, that I was shocked if someone actually said my name.

On the rare occasion I was allowed free reign, I shone. I volunteered to produce the school play *Cinderella* as it made no sense to me that this beautiful young girl could be treated so harshly by her ugly sisters. I re-wrote the script and turned it into a comedy, where Cinderella became the plucky, difficult, and offbeat character who gave her ugly sisters a hard time. Although I was scared that I would get into trouble for daring to change this sacred story, I took the lead role of Cinderella and everyone was stunned by my performance. They kept saying, "Who is this wild funny girl? That's not the quiet, shy Catherine we know!"

That experience boosted my confidence and I went on to become dux of the school, captain of the sports team, and head prefect. I thought I was the ants pants!

I was then dealt a devastating blow. In those days, you had to be a certain age to go to high school and as I was six months too young, I had to repeat a year. I had been with my close friends since kindergarten and excelling academically, so to be left behind whilst the rest of my class went to the Catholic college on the other side of town made me feel humiliated and unimportant.

That last year in primary school was tough. However, when I was finally in high school, I began to blossom again. The young Order of Mercy nuns were dynamic and adventurous and encouraged me to go for what I wanted. I won prizes for art and debating and I was the youngest student ever to reach the tennis tournament finals. I had a lead role in the school play and I excelled in classical piano studies. My confidence was growing and even boys were starting to notice me, which made me feel defiant and adventurous as I was taught to believe boys were of the devil!

Then my world was shattered again. My parents announced we were leaving my beloved home town to live in the city. I had this wonderful carefree life where my creativity and free spirit were encouraged and nurtured and now I had to attend school in a big city where I didn't know a single soul. Of course I know now that this move was unavoidable and my parents showed such courage in making that huge decision. For a fourteen year-old girl however, it was a sudden, dramatic, and mysterious move that turned my world upside down.

I experienced ridicule, isolation, and anonymity, and my country town accent was laughed at. No-one wanted to hear about my old life and I was considered to be *un-cool*, so I migrated to a quiet group of girls who clearly felt sorry for me. I also discovered there were limited options for my creative passions and again no one asked me what I wanted.

I quickly disconnected from school life and it was only my academic ability that got me through my final year.

Learning How Not to be Me

During my teens and twenties, the pressure of pretending to be someone I'm not demanded an outlet and I became argumentative, opinionated, and difficult. I rebelled against anyone who told me what to do and I started dating a rock star who was on drugs and living the high life. That rebellious period ended abruptly when I was seriously injured in a car accident and bedridden for several months. It seemed that whenever I began to live my own life, the Universe stopped me in my tracks. Taking risks and expressing my free spirit was clearly way too risky.

I sought safe haven in a steady relationship until I realized the life of a traditional wife wasn't for me. So I grabbed my backpack and went travelling around the world for two years. I felt liberated and totally in charge of my life, taking risks that now make my hair stand on end!

When I returned home, I allowed my family's conservative views sway me and I settled in to a dull and boring job until my restless spirit again tapped me on the shoulder. I talked my way into a role in the media with no experience and re-discovered my creativity and the confidence to take greater risks in my career.

I soon discovered I had a talent for public speaking and engaging people in a vision for their future and, although I was extremely successful and had a high profile, privately I was lonely. I was hiding out in full view and the harder I fought to be noticed and accepted, the more I attracted rejection and loneliness. I destroyed a loving relationship and kept choosing partners who were emotionally unavailable.

Just as I was giving up on finding a soul mate, I met the love of my life. Rob recognized my free and loving spirit and together we faced the next massive challenge: life in the corporate jungle.

Surviving in the Corporate Jungle

Given my experience in putting myself out there and being shut down, what on earth possessed me to persevere in corporate life? I obviously had more lessons to learn and the most profound was about *letting go*. This lesson was brutally brought home to me when I took a position with a company full of incompetent and self-serving managers. The fact that they called themselves the *leadership team* was laughable. Their priority was protecting their positions at all costs as they drowned in meaningless mission statements and vacuous values. Although it was clear that the company was in terminal disrepute, I remained determined to make a difference.

After ten years, something had to give, and that something was me. It took enormous energy to maintain a facade and I eventually exploded. I told management what I thought of them and ended up on stress leave feeling exhausted physically, mentally, and spiritually.

Then an amazing thing happened. I returned to find my office demolished and my belongings dumped in a box. Although I was hurt by this callous act, I soon realized it was a blessing and another signal to let go. I moved away from the psychopath in a suit who was wreaking havoc, to a different department with space to breathe.

The Gift

By letting go and putting my attention on me, I began to see that dramatic turn of events as a gift, and I attracted new experiences and new people into my life who recognized and nurtured my potential.

After attending a workshop on how to be successful in business followed by a life changing seminar, I woke up to the realization that *I* am in charge of my life; that it's OK to be who I am and no one can make me feel inadequate. I also learnt that I am special in the way that I can make a contribution.

Business coaching also enabled me to identify my passion for making a difference in the lives of others, particularly women. I was still in my corporate job, so it was tough and scary planning a new business and leaving behind a big salary for a leap into the unknown. The pain of staying in that toxic environment however was worse than the pain of leaving.

So I took the plunge and quit my job.

Shortly after I left, the organization was swallowed up by a competitor whom management always viewed with contempt (and clearly ignorance!). Now that's karma!

I then began running workshops with my business partner to inspire women looking for greater meaning in their lives, just like me. Once again I attracted what I needed to learn most about myself. Whilst the work was rewarding, I felt I wasn't fully expressing the contribution I wanted to make, as I still didn't know what that was!

I went on to establish a business providing environmental products for the home which connected me with entrepreneurial women who also wanted to make a difference. Although rewarding, it wasn't feeding my soul.

Discovering my Passions

Then I discovered an amazing tool called The Passion Test which helped me identify my top passions in life. This was a major breakthrough for me and for the first time ever I had complete clarity about what I wanted to do with my life.

The next challenge was to bring those passions alive so I trained as a Passion Test facilitator. With the guidance of my extraordinary business strategist, I tackled that old belief about feeling invisible by embracing it as a gift. I got to see that on some level, before I chose to step onto this planet, I decided I had to go through the pain of feeling invisible; of not being noticed, so I could be of service to women who are experiencing that same pain. Beth told me I would choose this life over and over so I can contribute in this way; that's how loving I am.

This blew me away! I had never had anyone acknowledge me in this way. She said these women have been waiting for me and they are showing up because I am ready for them. I understand their journey and I'm meeting them where they are. This is my life's work.

Your destiny is right there in your heart, waiting to be discovered. The world is waiting for you and your unique gifts. Are you ready to shine your light in the world?

My wish is that this story will touch a place in your heart and open you up to the infinite possibilities that await you.

About the Author

Cate McDonald is a motivational speaker and certified Passion Test facilitator. She specializes in guiding women to explore, embrace, and express their true essence through a gentle and transformational process of self-discovery and self-expression.

Cate has extensive experience in facilitating personal transformation and is passionate about making a difference in the lives of women around the world, including disadvantaged ones. Cate is also an ambassador for Life Aid International, a not-for-profit organization assisting developing nations in the areas of education, health, and micro-enterprise.

http://www.catemcdonald.com

THE SEARCH FOR HAPPINESS

Steve Martile

I wish life were easier. In 2005 I hit rock bottom. Well, at least I thought so.

I was in a job I hated, doing work I hated, and in a sixty-minute daily commute I hated. My life was headed in the wrong direction – that was for sure. I knew I had potential; that I could really do great things and impact the world. But sometimes knowing is simply not enough.

Financially, we were secure. I had a good-paying job and so did my wife. We had a nice home in a beautiful neighborhood and we had just started a little nest egg for our retirement.

But, boy was I ever unhappy!

I felt that something was missing, but if only I knew what. I needed to make some changes big time, so I started with the obvious. I had always dreamed of having a sports car. I love speed. So I bought a Nissan 350Z with 287 horsepower – all muscle.

The car was great and I loved it, but it was only a temporary patch. It felt nice to drive it, but something *bigger* was still missing. I thought the car would make me happy.

It didn't.

Truth #1: *Anytime you rely on the outside world to make you happy, you are working with a temporary solution. Do this often enough and you create a belief system – what I call the chasing mentality – chasing after the things you want to have because you think they will make you happy.*

I kept the Nissan 350Z for a few years. I drove it and enjoyed it, but I knew it wasn't part of my end game. I realized there must be something else, but what? That led to an important question, a sort of mantra that played in my head as I kept searching for happiness: *What are you passionate about and what do you want to do with your life?*

Then something caught my eye and grabbed my attention. It was something much bigger, and this time it wasn't a car. I got an idea for a tutoring business and I decided in that moment that I would tutor my way to success, or at least that is how I would start.

So I sold the sports car and put all of my attention into building this tutoring business part-time.

It was fun. I had tutored math when I was in high school and really enjoyed it, so getting paid to do the same thing wasn't much of a stretch.

At first, I started slow. There were a few bumps in the beginning, but I figured it out along the way. I even got a few paying clients. The income was nothing to call home about, but since I was still working as a full-time engineer I was able to take care of our living expenses and pay the bills.

As I started tutoring, I came to realize that these teenagers seemed flat; they seemed off and unhappy. "That's interesting," I thought. "Happiness should be a priority. Is there really anything else more important?"

That got me thinking about these kids and how I could help them. And with that thought came another and then another. Then a list of deep questions began to flow through me; questions like:

- What is it that you want?

- What are your goals over the next five years?

- What do you want to accomplish?

- What are your dreams?

- What do you want to do?

- What are you passionate about and what do you want to do with your life?

You must remember these kids were between thirteen and eighteen years of age and had never been asked these kinds of questions! In fact, most of them had never been asked what they wanted at all. They were always told what to do by their parents and teachers, so this lead to some big breakthroughs in a huge way. These kids finally got to share what they hoped and dreamed of.

One of my tutoring clients was a real star. His name was Matthew and he was so humble and quiet most of the time. After working with him for a few sessions and asking him those deep-felt questions, I discovered that he loved music, wrote music, and even had a band.

He was only fourteen years old. What potential!

I was on to something here. What started out as math tutoring once a week turned into coaching and tutoring twice a week. I let the parents know what I was doing and that they just had to pay me for the math tutoring. I would do the coaching part for free. And I kept asking my clients those same deep questions.

At the time, I wasn't sure if it was for my clients' benefit or mine, but asking the questions seemed to help and make me feel better, so I just went with it.

Truth #2: *Discovering who you are and what you're meant to be doing should not be a chore – it should be fun! The more fun you have, the better you feel. The better you feel, the happier you'll be. The happier you are, the greater the opportunities you attract. Listen to your feelings. They know the way.*

I kept rolling with the math tutoring. I was good at it and the kids (my clients) seemed to like it too. I did this for an entire year. Then suddenly, the tutoring and free-coaching didn't seem to feel right. There was still something missing and so I got the nudge again to go bigger.

Again, I was led back to this important question: "What are you passionate about and what do you want to do with your life?"

The more I asked this question, the better life got. So I kept asking in hopes of finding something better.

Then I got an idea; one that scared and excited me at the same time. I thought, "Why not create a coaching business and do it full-time?"

I decided to act on the idea. I still remember that day. I was terrified. I walked right into the CEO's office and told him that I was going to resign and start my own coaching business. I told him I was passionate about coaching and that I was also writing my very own blog. And what happened next floored me.

He gave me a big hug and congratulated me!

He even did one better. He said, "Steve, if you want, we'll hire you back as a consultant after your last day as a full-time employee – from that point forward you can work part-time as a consultant until you get your business up and running."

What a shock! I was elated. I was going to pursue my dream and be able to take care of my family. It was as if I had this magic wand and whenever I wanted something, I would just act on my ideas and the wand would waive its magic.

I was so happy. Life was good.

Truth #3: *When you get an idea, act! Don't delay. The Universe loves speed. Release the words, "I already know that" or "this won't lead to anything" from your mind. Just move towards your goals and your goals will indefinitely move towards you.*

I wish this was a fairytale ending, but it's not. The next sixteen months tell the story of my greatest struggle and lesson on my search for happiness.

As I was learning and trying to figure out how to make a good income from my coaching business, I hit another bleak reality. It was a Friday afternoon in Toronto, sixteen months after quitting my job and I went to review my bank statements for the first time in months.

- *Money Going Out Each Month = $6,000*

- *Money Coming In Each Month = $3,000*

Our Situation seemed hopeless. I was completely broke and going even more broke by the minute.

Then the breakthrough moment came. My moment of realization: I need to be financially responsible for my family and I need to do whatever it takes. I need to do that *now*!

So that's what I did. But my focus was not on the money. It was on making a contribution and giving openly. As I started to put my focus on others and what I could do to help them, I started to manifest some magical things – money and fabulous opportunities – so I kept waiving my wand.

Within a sixteen month period, I went from earning $1,000 monthly to $10,000 monthly and moved from a 1,600 sq.ft home into a beautiful 3,100 sq.ft one. I became financially responsible and I started to have more fun and feel really good about what I was doing. And most importantly, for the first time in my life, I felt I was living life on *my* terms. That life was up to *me*. And that brought me true satisfaction.

Truth #4: *When you contribute, you come alive. Contribution is the essence of your soul. When you contribute you unlock godly forces that bring a whirlwind of treasure back to you. Give openly and often.*

The truth is that you are the change you want to see and you can create whatever you want. If you want to be happy, you can create that too.

My purpose is this: to remind you that you are the co-creator. You are the wizard. You are the magician. You are the painter. You are the Picasso of your life. It's all you.

About The Author

Steve Martile is the creator and founder of Freedom Education. He began his search for happiness back in 2005 when he realized his life and his career were headed in the wrong direction. Steve is an engineering consultant, blogger and prosperity coach who inspires over ten thousand people monthly on his blog.

He lives in Sudbury, Canada, with his lovely wife Trisha and best buddy: his pooch, Chloe.

http://www.freedomeducation.ca

GUIDING FORCES

Cheryl Andrea

As a young child I noticed and began following the Angels' signals, just as Hansel and Gretel followed the breadcrumbs in the fairytale. I was fascinated with patterns that kept showing up. I was born on the twenty-seventh and had always considered it my personal number. So it made sense the angels would get my attention by using it. It wasn't that surprising that my entire life fell apart in 2007: the year with a big, loud, obvious 27 in it!

I had recommitted myself to serving in the highest forms possible and had made a personal vow to follow the Angels lead: *please, just show me the way*. I simply wanted to live my passion: to inspire and assist; to empower and uplift; to guide and to teach. I wanted joy again. I wanted to feel authentic and alive. I wanted freedom from the pain I was experiencing.

Not surprisingly, powerful shifts unfolded and led to a whole new life.

I was in my office in December 2006, and suddenly, I heard my guides gently whisper, "Go to the Dallas Psychic Fair. Your time is running out."

"But I'm already in private practice, why work the Fair?" I thought.

In response, they simply repeated, "Your time is running out..."

I have learned to pay attention to spiritual guidance, so I immediately called and the timing was perfect as their next event was days away. We set up an interview for me to become one of their professional readers and it went beautifully.

Several months later they contacted me again and, despite the long wait-list, had found a spot for me. I soon discovered why I had really been sent: the owners of twenty-five years announced they were looking for their successors! I knew with every fiber of my being that that was why my guides had led me there, so I would already be in place when the owners announced their decision. I had not even finished reading the announcement before I went running across the ballroom waving that pink postcard in the air.

"Bee, it's me! That's why my guides sent me here!" I shouted.

She laughed and calmly replied, "Well honey, you are the first one to step forward. We will have to speak with all interested parties. We are not in a hurry. We are more interested in finding the right people for the business."

She went on to outline a few things and then looked directly in my eyes and said, "We do need to know: Do you have the money?"

She went on to share their sales price and terms - one wire transfer for the entire asking price with no financing whatsoever!

Now let me say this...not once, up to that point, did it occur to me that I would be buying a business. I know it may sound ridiculous, but I was so overcome with gratitude, for all God and the Universe had obviously orchestrated, that I hadn't yet considered what it all meant for my life at the time.

I had not yet internalized *any* of it.

After meeting with the sellers once and waiting two months for their call, they finally offered me a formal invitation to buy the business. They had interviewed eight different parties and stated with surprise: "You were right. It *is* you!"

As we set a timeline for the transition and take-over of the business, amazing things continued to occur...

I told everyone I knew I was buying the Fair and asked whether they, or someone they knew, might be interested in providing a high-interest, short-term loan. The first woman who committed, offered to fund half what I had asked for. I agreed! I saw her offering a portion of the money as an indication that I was heading where I wanted to go, and so I remained faithful.

With a sense of empowerment, I shared my progress and observations with a group of lunch friends, some whom I barely knew at the time. One woman approached me after our lunch and offered her financial support. She explained she dreamed of assisting women entrepreneurs and was inspired by my story. She wanted to be a part of what I was creating.

The next woman who joined our project was a referral from an acquaintance. We had never spoken before and neither of us had heard of the other until the day I called her. In less than ten minutes, she said, "Cheryl, I have never done such a thing, but I am going to tell you yes! I feel so good about supporting your project. I will have a cashiers' check for you the day after tomorrow."

There were three other significant investors who assisted with the acquisition funds, one who agreed to a loan after I asked a second time (months later) because I told her I had raised all but fifteen thousand.

The night before the wire transfer to the sellers was to be made, we were a mere five thousand dollars short. I called a friend and asked for his advice regarding how I should inform them. Generously, he responded, "I will lend you the five thousand. Don't worry about interest or terms. Just repay me later. Cheryl, I believe in you!"

Every person who participated said those words to me. And every single dollar arrived on time.

As my professional life was blossoming, my marriage was disintegrating. I acknowledged that I had not yet learned how to maintain my focus - to remember my purpose - amidst the daily chaos and anger that existed in my environment. I handed the matter over to the Angels. I was done. I had given my best, fought my hardest, and ultimately discovered true peace could only be found by letting go.

Soon after that day of surrendering, my youngest son and I were to attend a party for his soccer coach. I was not feeling social or interested in having small talk with soccer parents I didn't know well. I considered not going when I heard my guides direct me. "You must go," they said.

"Why?" I asked.

"You'll see."

Only minutes after we arrived, a group of moms were asking the coach's wife questions about their upcoming transfer overseas.

"So what are you doing with your house while you're in Malaysia?" one mom asked.

"Well, that's the funny thing. We had a guy who was going to take care of it for us, but he called this morning and said he'd changed his mind."

I was stunned. I could feel every hair on my body stand in attention. In that moment I saw clearly why my guides had insisted that I go to the party. I also knew in an instant, the outcome of my marriage and it made me angry. I had been holding onto the idea that God was going to show me how to save my marriage. Now I had been let in on this secret, and shown another step in the grand plan.

I was not happy about it.

Knowing that taking any action in that state would not serve anyone well, I took time to process my feelings until I accepted where I was being led. Once I had, I called the coach and offered to assist them by caring for their property while they were away. I explained that my children and I were about to go through a divorce and needed to stay in our community for my oldest son to graduate in two years.

"Could it be the solution for both of us?" I asked.

Amazingly enough, they agreed. But the most astounding part is that their only request was that I keep the utilities in their name and manage those bills! No rent? Incredible! I could not have known to ask for such an arrangement. God, the Universe, and the Angels had it *all* handled.

When I left my husband, I had two children, two dogs, and myself to provide a new life for. We were moving into someone else's home for an undetermined time with no idea where we would go next. And my bank account had only $79 in it. All this occurred while I was buying a business I had no idea why I was being led to buy, and with other people's money!

We stayed in their home for two and a half years. During which I discovered the Universe had much more to reveal as I showed up with eagerness to learn.

My private practice shifted into high gear and in new directions. The Fair was my second business and one that was paying for itself over the first thirty months, as I used nearly all profits to repay the investors who believed in me. Producing the Fair each month provided an education, not an income, so managing my private practice was imperative to support my family.

Furthermore, I had determined that in order to disentangle myself from any encumbrances of my old life, I had to let go of all expectations of others, especially my husband. If he chose to pay child support and hold regular visitation, it would be entirely up to him. I was neither going to ask him for support of his children nor would I enforce it either. I had to be free to choose new things; not be controlled by the old. Despite the many unknowns I was facing, I was guided to take it on!

Throughout my life, I have been driven by the deep knowing that I was given free will; and that life is creative and full of choices. I am willing to risk and to believe in greater and grander versions than what is evident in this moment. It makes life a grand adventure. I know this is my purpose: to live authentically and openly; to teach others to live an empowered life led by the unseen.

All of us can access Divine intelligence by heightening our awareness and learning to perceive our environment differently than we've been previously taught.

All of us have a direct connection to the unseen world from which we have come. We must simply re-member ourselves!

These experiences taught me valuable tools that perhaps you too, will find useful for creating an empowered life. I learned (with a couple bumps and bruises along the way) that:

1. All the contrast and discomfort in my life served me well to determine what I wanted and to commit to creating it. I wanted to experience life authentically and fully. What is uncomfortable in your life that may be helping you define your soul's greater desires?

2. How to become more response-able in managing my energy. Instead of trying to control my environment or people in it, I remained clear about my connection to Source and mind-

ful I was creating my future by where I focused my attention. I didn't waste energy concerning myself with why, when, where, through whom, or how an end result would be achieved. I left that to God, the Universe, and the Angels who have a better view of more than this slice of time. What one thing could you let go of right now that would stop wasting energy you could use to create a more meaningful life experience?

3. How to become more observant of self. I discovered our discomfort or pain is not about the *other person* or the environment; it is always derived from how we perceive *our experience*. I acknowledged that I did not have all the answers and did not judge myself for where I was. What do you repeatedly judge about yourself? How would you feel if you stopped?

4. To deliberately choose to find good in each moment and to view my current experience as being directed by something greater than me. Only then was I able to relax enough in faith to see opportunities as they were revealed to me. Do you feel connected to something greater than yourself? Do you choose to look for the good in your experiences?

5. To redirect my attention by reiterating my vow *to serve* anytime I felt fear or confusion. Re-membering myself by focusing on all I appreciated in any given moment brought me to a state of presence every time. Once present, new possibilities became apparent and forward movement could be granted. How often do you relax and observe the moment you're in? Do you choose to feel appreciation and wonder?

6. To remain present, as a participant in each part of the experience. Each time I asked for something, it was like pitching a ball to the Universe. I waited to see the next indication. Do I run to first base? Do I stay? Am I almost home? How well are you interacting with the Universe? Are you trying to micromanage their job?!

About the Author

Cheryl is a multi-generational clairvoyant, clairaudient, and medium who has experienced communication with other dimensions since early childhood. Over the years, her *human experiences* have varied greatly with lessons in compassion, judgment, tolerance, understanding, and love. She has developed an intense appreciation for being consciously aware and response-able in her life, and knows her purpose is assisting others in awakening to higher truths and living an empowered and joyous life.

Cheryl has been professionally reading for clients since 1997, although she's had a lifelong experience of receiving information from other dimensions for the benefit of healing on all levels: spiritually, mentally, emotionally, and physically.

Cheryl is also the owner and producer of Dallas Psychic Fair, a monthly event held on the first Sunday of each month as well as co-founder of Psychic YOUniverse.

http://www.cherylandrea.com

AWAKENING TO YOUR SOUL'S PURPOSE

Michelle Locke

Think of those two important words: *passion* and *purpose*. They could be written together as *passionate purpose* or *purposefully passionate* or even *passionately purposeful*. In whichever way you put them together they are the very qualities that give life meaning.

Passion I describe is the feeling of intense emotional energy. It is the driving force, the energy of love within us. Purpose is the call of the soul to live this energy in our daily life. Life force is the invisible energy common to all things that connects us to the oneness. We call this oneness many things: God, Consciousness, the Tao, and the Self to name just a few. It is all the same thing, called by a multitude of different names depending on our cultural and spiritual beliefs.

When we are able to meaningfully express our selves as love, we align with the purpose of our soul, which is to remember our connection to oneness. There are as many ways to do this as there are humans on this earth! There *is* no right or wrong way to do anything. As long as we are living from our authentic heart the best way we can in this moment, we will be purposefully aligned.

Asking questions of ourselves can assist us to stay purposefully aligned in our lives. They can help us to review and reflect on where we are living authentically in our lives and where we are not. Indicators of good times to ask these questions are the times when we feel unsure of where we are in our life, unhappy with what we are doing, or blaming our life situation for how we are feeling. These are opportunities to bring ourselves back into alignment with our path through life. Some of the questions I often ask myself are:

1. What do I love?

2. What am I passionate about?

3. What nurtures my heart?

4. What is my deepest soul desire?

These questions may seem simple, but they work to keep me focused and living authentically. They bring me back to the present; to what is important to me now and how I am feeling at a deep level. When the little things threaten to overwhelm me as I get caught up in the busyness of life, answering these questions brings immediate clarity and help.

My work as the creator of Wu Tao Dance would not be possible without passion. Wu Tao is a dance process similar to Tai Chi and Yoga, which balances the life force energy in the body. It is beautiful to do and it works to relieve emotional stress and physical imbalances. People often ask me how I came up with Wu Tao and what made me to want to create it. What drove me was a deep love for humanity coupled with a very strong desire to be of service. I believe we are all connected and every person I see is a part of me. We are not separate from each other. When I see suffering in another, I know that I am suffering at some level too. We all need healing. By offering love and healing to others I am offering it to myself! When I teach Wu Tao to others, I am giving the benefits to myself!

Of course I have plenty of moments and experiences where I don't live from this understanding, especially when another person shows a particularly 'ugly' side of human nature that I would prefer not to own. However, I choose to treat myself kindly by offering love when I can and being gentle on myself when I am struggling to love.

My life experiences have helped me align with my purpose. It's not easy to understand that we have set in motion all the events in our life. This demands responsibility and the moving out of feeling like a victim in any and every way. However, once I began doing this in small ways at first, the Universe did seem to go out of its way to help me.

A long time ago, I was drifting through my life, unsure of what I wanted to do or where to go. I was lost, depressed, and very sad. I had stopped dancing for the ballet company I was in, due to a serious back injury. Dancing had been my whole life. I was eight years old when I decided I was going to become a ballerina.

Then it was all taken away from me in a heartbeat because of this injury.

I remember picking up Louise Hay's little blue book subtitled *The Mental Causes for Physical Illness* around this time. *What a concept!* This was so alien to me that after reading it I threw it at the wall in utter disbelief and horror. The idea that my thoughts were creating my dis-ease was unbelievable and yet something rang true. I frantically tried all the affirmations for back problems hoping the pain would disappear overnight. Unfortunately it didn't, but a seed had been sown in my mind: the possibility that there was another way of looking at things that could help me heal my back.

The small beginnings of true self responsibility.

I believe I co-created numerous difficult situations for myself to grow and evolve. To name a few, I had to give up a career that I loved through injury, I had been married and divorced twice, I had experienced the difficulties of being a single parent to two beautiful daughters, my youngest daughter Isabelle was severely disabled with Rett syndrome, and, most recently, I had to go through the incredibly painful and devastating experience of losing her when she chose a transition out of this world.

While it would have been only too easy to be a victim through these experiences (don't worry; I tried!), I discovered that taking responsibility for having created these experiences gave me the opportunity to grow and expand. Taking responsibility doesn't mean beating yourself up. That can happen when you judge something as bad.

For example, my daughter had a disability. How did I create this (bad) situation? If I saw this as *my fault* and *bad* I will probably give myself a hard time and feel guilty, hopeless and bad. Taking responsibility means understanding that this experience is in my field of awareness to help me grow in some way.

A course in miracles states it like this: "Everything that happens to me, I have called for." This is a very difficult idea to come to terms with. An easy way to practice this is to open and embrace everything you encounter in your life. Instead of resisting, blaming, or fighting what is in your path, just embrace it and use it to become more of your self.

When my daughter Belle first began showing symptoms of Rett syndrome including losing her ability to talk, walk, and hold things with her hands, my life took a major turn. As you can imagine this was a very challenging time. Deep grief coupled with intense worry and anxiety were the major flavor of these difficult few years. It was very hard to surrender but trust and surrender was the practice that got me through.

Have you ever had the feeling that everything you have done has led you to a certain place? This is what happened to me. There was this little space of time where I wasn't able to work because of my sick child and because of an intense period of stress and grief. I found myself sincerely praying for guidance and help for my life.

What came through shortly after was the beginning of my life work, the inspiration and ideas for Wu Tao.

Within the space of a few short months, I choreographed a sequence of five dances, developed a series of meditations, wrote a book, and started teaching Wu Tao to anyone willing to try it. I had no idea where it was going, but Wu Tao (which means *the dancing way*) took off like wild fire in my home city. Within a few years I was travelling the country teaching and training people in the healing dance method of Wu Tao.

Many people have suggested that Wu Tao is channeled information. I agree to a point, in that it is channeled from a different aspect of my self. However channeled information can imply separation. *It came from out there, from another dimension and I am here.* It's true, my little self may be here on this planet seemingly running the show, but the rest of me, (the part that is also one with you!) is a creative genius with marvelous powers and I was simply able to tune in to that higher self for a time. My passion for people and desire for healing, combined with prayerful intention, allowed me to connect with an expanded part of the self or oneness and create Wu Tao.

My story isn't that unique. I have journeyed through many difficult places and I have ended up here. What I now appreciate about the perfection of life is that my experiences, whether I viewed them as positive or negative, have led me to where I am now. I have discovered that the quicker I surrender to an experience, the easier I am able to grow and evolve and the less suffering there is.

When I reflect on the past I see the incredible intelligence of life working behind the scenes to wake me up. When I take full responsibility for what is happening to me in my life;s mirror, I change and the world changes with me. Taking responsibility allows me to live my life on purpose, deliberately and consciously choosing how to be, think, act, and respond.

Just for a moment reflect on your own life. Can you stand back and view it from a distance? What parts of yourself are you up against? Where is life working for you? How is your soul calling to you?

Once you know you are the creator of your life, once you truly know you are responsible, then *everything* that happens to you becomes an opportunity to awaken and evolve. This is the path of purposeful living. If you choose to be a victim, that is, to blame the outside for what is happening to you, your deep purpose will remain hidden from view.

The outcome of *not* taking responsibility is the creation of crisis in some form, to *force* deep inner transformation and growth. There is absolutely nothing wrong or bad with crises apart from the suffering part. Crises simply create opportunities to view situations from another vantage point and evolve.

Devolving is moving in the direction set in motion by resisting the situation and blaming the outside. It constricts the flow of energy and ties it up in a knot. The outcome of viewing a situation from this perspective could mean an increase in stress and anxiety, a deadening of life force, illness, or depression.

Evolving is the process of going with the flow of energy, knowing that the situation is there to enable growth. Each one of us has a higher aspect of our selves guiding us through our life on earth. It's like an invisible thread constantly with us through every experience in our lives. It's not always obvious, but it's there and this thread is always pulling us towards the expression of our highest purpose and evolution. Choosing to evolve brings you more of what you are: more love, joy, and energy!

Purposeful living is not finite. It's not something that ends like a job. Purpose is your soul calling you home to your self, to your true nature! Every moment lived on purpose by following the flow of love and passion within you is an awakening. This is the real gift of living on this earth.

My sincere prayer is that all human beings come to remember this truth.

About the Author

Michelle Locke is the creator and founder of Wu Tao Dance, a healing therapy that balances life force energy. A professional ballerina in the early 80's, Michelle went on to study Shiatsu and Chinese medicine after sustaining a serious back injury which ended her career.

Since its inception in 2001, Wu Tao is now taught by licensed instructors to hundreds of people worldwide and is enjoyed by people of all age groups. Michelle lives with her partner Steve Richter, who composes all the original music for Wu Tao and with whom she has recently created Wu Tao for couples which helps to facilitate deep intimacy and connection in relationships.

Michelle Locke is an inspiring educator and dancer who is dedicated to improving the physical and spiritual health of people everywhere. She is the mother of two beautiful daughters; her youngest, Isabelle, who had Rett syndrome, passed away in 2011.

http://www.wutaodance.com

REFLECTIONS IN THE SKY

Aan Frazier

My story starts with the beautiful moon. As a silent witness that floats quietly in the grand sky, he has observed me grow into the person that I am today. It is through this lovely rock in the sky that I will delicately tell my story of passion and purpose.

Ever since I was a little girl, I have always adored the moon. Peering from my window on warm summer nights, he would look down on me with his gentle glare. I loved every line and every crater about his face; they were so full of character, which made my imagination run wild. Could it be true? Was he really made of cheese? Although limited in his colors, he would always somehow find ways to present himself differently and in many shades. Best of all, the moon was always swifter than any bird I knew. I remember the moon always beating us home on late nights when my dad drove. I always wondered how he was able to do it, but could not care less how he managed to; I just loved him with all my heart.

As I grew older, life changed and I often forgot about my bright shape in the sky. The buzzes of day and daily demands of life rarely gave me the luxury of just staring wonderingly into the sky anymore. Typical were the nights when I crashed into bed in order to recuperate from sleep deprivation. Because of this, the moon was always nowhere to be found. In my world, he did not even exist anymore.

Then one difficult day, life felt suffocating and I had nowhere else to go but outside in the dark night to take a breather. As I did this, the thought of my beloved moon re-entered my mind. It had been quite some years but the memory of him warmed my heart. In a tired frenzy, I searched for that familiar warm gaze again. I longed to see the same face that brought me so much joy as a child. When I finally found him hidden behind some trees, my eyes rested upon a face that was surprisingly different.

This strange moon looked plain and gray. His glow was dimmed and he lacked the luster that was once there. I stared at him more intensely, trying to see if my eyes were playing tricks on me. The more I looked, the grimmer the reality was that my beloved moon was no longer the same. As I walked back to my house, I thought I glimpsed a scowl on his face as I took one last glance. I thought, "Yikes, he does not like me anymore!"

Similar were the nights that followed this strange meeting with the moon. I would find myself stepping outside into the night during any hard obstacle or any growing pain I was going through. Though hopeful in being reunited with the same moon that I once knew, I would time and time again, be greeted by his same uninviting glow.

Where was that beautiful face that I had once loved? Part of me started to dismiss my old memory of him; thinking that it must have been my naïve and childish imagination. I began to accept this plain moon as the true moon in my current reality.

On many of those dreary nights of staring into this *real* moon and reflecting on my woes, I found myself drifting back to another familiar but bittersweet memory. It was the memory of the hardest year of my life retold by my parents, and the moon was right there to witness it all. The hardest year in my life was my first year of life and the memory goes as follows.

Through hopes and miracles, I am a surviving refugee of the infamous Vietnam War. Born after the fall of Saigon, my parents wanted a better life for me and my sister above the destruction and chaos. Their first attempt was unsuccessful; they were incarcerated. My mother, pregnant with me at the time, received an early release because of her expecting condition. Because of her traumatic experience and lack of nutrition, I was born a small and weak baby. To this day, the back of my head is flat; evidence that my feeble infant body lay still on my mother's wooden bed for hours at a time.

My father was finally released and I grew stronger. My parents attempted to leave again by giving up more gold bars and embarking on another secret plan. They successfully boarded a small fisherman's boat, squeezed in with ninety other refugees. In the dark cloak of night, they shed all that they knew of their previous lives as they sailed on into an uncertain, but hopeful, future.

What was supposed to be a three-day journey turned into a fourteen-day ordeal due to merciless waves and a broken motor. Also unexpected were the repeated pirate attacks against our boat which only held meager belongings. My mother recalls trying to salvage one last piece of jewellery by hiding it in her mouth from the searching pirates!

Through the entire trip, my mother kept me close. Holding me firmly in her arms, the only protection I had was her fearful embrace and a blanket of undeveloped awareness at twelve months old. I only had the understanding of basic needs. As food supplies ran out and starvation kicked in, she recalls that I repeatedly patted her cheek and then mine. With no more food to give, she ignored me and I eventually ceased to ask. The life-saving rain became our breakfast, lunch, and dinner.

My father retells of the final horrific pirate attack that almost buried us at sea. Riding in on two large ships and armed with weapons, we had no chance against the thieves. After robbing us, the two pirate ships decided to drift alongside on either side of our tiny boat. Then they merged together with the intention of crushing us into a thousand pieces. My dad recalls thinking that that was it; that we were all going to die right there and then. He squinted his eyes and braced for the impact. Miraculously, they missed our boat and scuffed one another. As if our boat was under Divine protection, they left us alone and moved on in search for new destructive play.

As this memory slowly faded and started to leave my mind, the sight of the moon in front of me started to sharpen, and I took a deep breath and sighed as the memory comes to a positive conclusion.

Through our shaken spirits and ribs showing through tattered clothes, we made it to Indonesia and eventually the United States where I grew up to be a healthy adult. Ironically, I am the strongest of five siblings. I have been blessed, but something has always eluded me.

Growing up as a first generation Asian American, I took the path that was laid out for me by my parents: to do well in school, go to college, and land a great job. I had graduated with honors and had become a dedicated teacher. Inspiring young minds, twenty a time, for the past ten years has brought me great satisfaction.

But still, I wanted more.

Given an extraordinary second chance at life, I wanted to do extraordinary things for myself and the world. I felt like there was a void that needed to be filled in the Universe and it had my name on it. I wanted to fill this void for myself, my parents, and perhaps a higher being. The only problem was, I did not know what I would do or how I would do it.

I was lost about this for years until I stumbled upon something called the Law of Attraction six years ago. Skepticism and curiosity turned into enlightenment and empowerment as knowledge of the Law of Attraction changed my life in an electrifying way. The simple idea that *we become what we think about* has in a way, defibrillated my brain into a new vibrational direction. My mind, a powerful and precious possession, held the key to all my questions all along. This significant change of awareness has ignited my soul and placed me on the path of fulfilling my dreams.

More than ever, I understand that attitude and perception are the powerful lenses to our own realities. The moon has been, and will always be, the same moon in the sky. How we perceive and feel about it will depend on what we have learned and what we choose to believe. For instance, the superstitious person will see a powerful moon and the *trick-or-treater*, an eerie one. I, for one, was merely seeing a plain and dim moon because of my own lackluster thoughts.

Today I live a different life filed with a different kind of thinking and attitude. I am in control of creating my reality and I believe that anything is possible. When I step outside now to take a breather, I do so purely to enjoy the night. When my eyes search for my bright shape in the sky, I no longer think of my woes. Life is too short to put focus on what is wrong. When I finally find him, I am no longer greeted by a plain dim glow. Instead, I am welcomed with a bright and magnificent face that lights up the entire night sky. Gratitude emanates from my being as I think about how lucky I am to be alive and to be in possession of pair of working eyes to view such a sight.

Today when I look up at the moon, I feel inspiration as my mind plays around with a few mind boggling facts. Amazing opportunities are out there for us to grab regardless of our situations and where we live, for we are all under the same moonlit sky governed by the same natural laws. Abundant opportunities will be brought into focus only when we allow for our minds to embrace them. I also relish in the outstanding thought that the same exact moon was shining down on the Ancient Egyptians and Byzantine Empire as it did for Thomas Edison and Princess Diana. And now it is shining down on me. The moon nudges me to think: if others can accomplish great things under this very same sky, why can't I?

Although now all grown up, I have often sensed that same magical wonder I felt as child when I stare lovingly at my rock in the sky in the evening. In fact, on a recent night, I was peering happily at him from my bedroom window, just as I did when I was a little girl. As I turned off the light and shuffled into bed to retire for the day, I could still see him beaming brightly from where I was laying on my pillow. He looked absolutely stunning. And just as I was about to fall asleep and before my eyes blinked for one last time, I thought I saw my beloved moon stretch a wide grin across his magnificent cratered face in every creative shade of gray imaginable.

He must have been proud of what he saw.

About the Author

Aan Frazier is a Vietnamese American, surviving refugee of the Vietnam War and author of *Your Sticky Mind*. Her family relocated to United States in California where she grew up and became an elementary school teacher. With a multiple subject credential and BA in child development, Aan has been teaching grades K-3 for the past ten years.

Life was *as usual* until Aan started learning the Law of Attraction. Recently, she has decided to take her knowledge and apply it towards her big dream of becoming a published author. With an elementary education background, she plans to inspire others by explaining the Law of Attraction using simple words and clear explanations. Aan's amazing journey which includes a blog, book trailer, and instructional YouTube videos, can be found on her website.

http://www.aanfrazier.com

PASSION FLOWER POWER

Deborah Kelley

My latest passion, which gives meaningful purpose to my life, occurred when I laid down my paintbrushes and began painting words with a dimension of life just beyond the five senses.

Another passion of mine is living victoriously by never playing victim. My new non-fiction work is based upon mental alchemy and the fourth Hermetic principle that states, "Everything is dual; everything has poles: pairs of opposites." This chapter reflects the empowering result of *living* this principle.

I'm delighted to share a few snapshot moments with you, when my spoken words, full of heartfelt intention for betterment, were wingless, until mystery visited. Being a lucid dreamer, conscious or unconscious, my life is never boring or empty. An awakened and watchful inner eye helps my spirit pay attention to both my conscious and unconscious mind's thoughts and words to bring manifestation into my life in a positive manner.

Every day, in my sixth decade of life, I see dozens of inspiring ways to live in the positive and brush away the negative. For example, I do not take hold of the fear of aging. This keeps me feeling and looking younger than my calendar years. One day, my oldest grandson was watching me apply lipstick. He said, "Grangran, does your skin get loose when you grow old?" I smiled and said, "Yes, but I'm so lucky mine still fits." He hesitated before pointing out a spot on my face that he thought looked loose. I laughed for days, but dabbed cream on my neck every time I passed a mirror.

Joy and acceptance have the power to neutralize all negativity. A day of stress and powerless living is what a beloved friend calls *the inability to embrace that which is before you.* All life circumstances, imaginings, and sudden synchronicities are opportunities to awaken to what you might be unconsciously manifesting. All lower vibrations, like stress or the fear of aging, are capable of being transformed by a powerful vibration of loving peaceful acceptance.

Before I began writing this piece on *passion and purpose,* I kept seeing a Passion Flower in my mind's eye. At first, I discerned the meaning of this snapshot vision as an indication to add this plant to my perennial flowerbed. I ordered a purple-blue vine species, a color my seven year-old granddaughter calls the color of peace. Yet, all during my writing, this puzzling image of a Passion Flower stayed with me. One morning I awoke and oddly associated this vision with Joseph Campbell's words regarding one of mankind's deepest purposes and challenges. He felt it was vitally important to seek a way to *joyfully participate in the sorrows of the world.*

Metaphorically, the Passion Flower, with its lovely fleshy petals, its frilly tentacle skirt, and antenna-like crown of thorns center, mirrors the multi-layered expressions of life; the physical body, emotional body, and the God seed center. All parts of this exotic plant, like the wholeness of being, possess extraordinary powers and are in fact, well-known as an effective natural treatment for anxiety. This vision infused me with inspiration and direction; however, it also brought flashes of painful true-life dramas associated with illness and anxiety back to me.

Following the 9/11 terrorist attacks on the United States, being a mother of a brave soldier fighting battles on foreign soil, stress was my constant companion. In contrast to my son's warrior nature, I am a flower-child from the 60's. During this time, I tumbled into profound grief. My baby boy, a brilliant graduate of a military academy, was sent to war.

Soon after my son's deployment, I was diagnosed with a stress-related disease called IBS (Irritable Bowel Syndrome). Against my strong belief of knowing the power of my words and thoughts in the process of healing, I felt victimized and powerless.

Despite these feelings, I continued seeking natural ways to heal my body. One book I read faithfully was titled *You Can Heal Your Life,* by Louise L. Hay. I learned from her a new thought pattern to help me battle my painful illness. I repeated daily, "I digest and assimilate all new experiences peacefully and joyously."

These remedy words poured out of my mouth without much power to combat my deep felt hatred for the horrifying reality of war. Compulsively, I ate out of comfort and watched the nightly war updates on the news. My son was a pilot. Every time a helicopter crashed, I anxiously awaited a knock at my door. Then, late one night, from a faraway place, I heard my son's voice call out to me in a pain-filled, guttural way: "Mama."

I rose from my bed and my knees hit the floor. Tears poured from my eyes. I began to tremble. I could hardly breathe, but even worse, I didn't want to. My son needed me and I wasn't there to comfort him. "Oh God," I cried, "Please don't take my boy from me. Take me!"

A Biblical scene came to my mind of a woman begging Jesus to speak the word and her child would be healed. An immediate healing manifested with this vision. I became that woman, begging Jesus for healing.

Eventually, I begged myself into a restless comma. No sooner were my eyes closed when I entered a lucid state of consciousness. I shot out of my bed like a rocket and experienced astral travel. I had experienced this before on rare occasions, but somehow this event felt different.

Within seconds, I landed abruptly into a misty white cotton candy world. Sitting in a circle around me, deep in quiet contemplation, sat nine yogis. Each wore a white turban atop their bowed heads. As I watched, their peace began to enter my body like liquid love. Simultaneously, I heard a thundering voice of great authority bellow forth these words: "I heard you the first time!"

Suddenly, I was back in bed, my eyes swollen from a night of tearful begging. I felt an unfamiliar humility and peace bubbling up inside of me. Humbled by a love that hears before I speak, who was I to demand special attention? My heart was at peace, because I no longer felt separate from my son or the God of my faith. Like Carl G. Jung said: "I don't believe in God, I know God." He knew himself inside and out, and I knew that I was on this same journey of Divine discovery.

This *knowing* of God, and myself, was rich food for my body and the breath my soul needed to powerfully blossom, even in the midst of great disharmony and chaos. I later learned that my son was safe, but was involved in a recent crisis. Through all this, I still had much work to do in order to completely resolve my health issue.

While seeking holistic ways to cure myself, I met a yogi master. He first appeared to me in a dream so real I reached out to touch him. He felt solid. I screamed. Soon I recognized this dear soul in wakeful life. I asked him if, in spirit, he knocked one night at my bedroom door. He smiled and answered, "Yes. The student doesn't always recognize their teacher."

One day I shared my many visions with him. He listened intently with his eyes closed. As I completed my stories, he spoke. "Mastery consists not of visions or fantastic images. These fade with time. When you can look out that window and love that tree as your brother, aha... that is progress."

Puzzled, I looked out his living room window at a tall evergreen tree. Suddenly, a strong emotion rose up from deep within my spirit. I looked at this tree as if I'd never seen a tree before. My mind emptied of everything, but this tree. I felt pressure building behind my eyes. Uncontrollable tears tumbling down my cheeks. I looked towards my teacher feeling shocked and embarrassed. "I'm sorry," I said, "I've just fallen madly, passionately in love with your tree."

He threw back his head, laughed, and clapped his hands. Somehow, I suspected he was a part of making this unfamiliar love manifest. It reminded me of the liquid peace I'd felt when my heavenly yogis were silently praying. "Now," my teacher laughed, still clapping and smiling, "you are making progress."

Three months later, my teacher's work on Earth was complete. He was a remarkable man, living well into his eighties with impressive, perfect eyesight. Our meeting showed me that, often, a peaceful death is the highest form of healing, but when the possibility of death came visiting me last summer, I did not embrace it with my teacher's peace. An annual medical test showed that tumors were growing on both my ovaries. Immediate surgery was recommended and I was referred to a cancer specialist.

Sitting in the doctor's office, the waiting room was overflowing with young women in various stages of hair loss. My heart overflowed with compassion and an overwhelming feeling of being tremendously blessed. If I were to die, it would be okay, because my children were already grown and had blessed me with five healthy grandchildren. I had a loving husband to stand by my side, but I wanted to live more of my life. I knew that there were still many buckets full of life awaiting my arrival.

Driving home, I was wondering how I'd make it through the next five days of not knowing if cancer cells were taking over my body. I hesitated in using prayer to remove my tumors for some unknown reason. As my car stereo played a soulful melody, I recalled a recent spirit encounter while visiting Lake Titicaca in Peru.

At the time, I thought I had a terrible case of altitude sickness. I missed a day of touring, drifting in and out of a heavy sleep. Suddenly, standing directly in front of me was a dark skinned man, box-like in stature. My first impression was that he was an Indian shaman or trickster spirit. Atop his head was a fur-lined headdress with buffalo horns sticking out where his ears should have been. To my own amazement, I was not frightened; only puzzled. Suddenly, he said, "I have two rooms you would die for."

I stood my ground and replied, "No thanks."

The next morning marked our last bus trip. I felt queasy and confused about my vision. Paradoxically, all day my husband and fellow travellers commented on how good I looked. Still puzzled, that night I asked the Universe for the root cause of my lingering nausea. In a half-sleep moment of consciousness, I heard a serene clairaudient voice whisper, "Centuries of pain."

Arriving home one day from a doctor appointment, I kept thinking of my Peruvian buffalo-man's words, *"He had two rooms I would die for,"* and my response, *"No thanks."* Through my imagination, I viewed my two ovaries as nursery rooms. These rooms were about to be removed, because my wise gynecologist insisted on yearly pelvic sonograms. My words, *"No thanks,"* and the word *would* gave me faith that I *would* not die. Not yet.

I began to imagine motherly fears and worries, collectively and personally, as a deep root cause of *centuries of pain* in womanhood. When my son was at war, my empathic pain grew daily. I could feel the pain for other mothers who were less fortunate than me. For my own good of returning to a healthy body state, I needed to drain this lingering pain from my body. I had to reach for the passion I once had for healing love. I was not ready to die, for I still had a purpose to fulfill.

Regardless of what the outcome would be, I was determined to remain at peace. I was ready to embrace whatever life would give me with a deeper understanding of the Divine law of cause and effect. In my Louise Hay's self-healing book, her remedy for cancer echoed my *centuries of pain* answer: "I lovingly forgive and release all of the past. I choose to fill my world with joy. I love and approve of myself". My passion would run deep into every energy source of my inner self."

I began a prayer-like meditation using higher vibrations of love and gratitude, to win victory over lower vibrations of sorrow and pain. With my eyes closed, gathering all my shadow-thoughts of sufferings, disbelief, anger, resentment, regret, guilt, and all things associated with pain into my arms and released it. I pictured Mother Mary wrapping her arms around me. I cannot even describe the love I felt awakening from surgery with news that my tumors benign. I was cancer free.

Recently, my six-year-old granddaughter said, "Grangran, Mother Mary is really strong. I saw a picture of her holding a grownup Jesus. She was sitting. He looked really heavy."

I smiled for days.

I give you this simple Celtic prayer-poem by Julian of Norwich. It reads: "Behold, I am the ground of thy beseeching." Now, without delay, stand firm upon this ground and grow *Passion Flower Power*.

About the Author

Deborah Kelley's paintings, as a visionary artist, display her love of nature and always incorporate a touch of the divine feminine. Her lifetime body of work includes oils, watercolor, pen and ink, and commercial illustration. At an early age, Deborah often experienced lucid states of dreaming, conversing with deceased loved ones and electrifying archetypal figures. Upon awakening, she often felt confused about what was real and what was unreal. From this fertile ground, her inner author awoke. Deborah's desire is to paint with words, from a Southern woman's perspective, a rich and beautiful dimension of life beyond the five senses.

http://www.deborahlkelley.com

WINGS OF LOVE

Denise O'Brien

I peeked at my mother as she stood in our kitchen crying because her beloved birds had escaped the backyard aviary. "Who opened the bird cage?" she quivered.

My siblings and I looked at each other in horror. How could we help Mom who had so tenderly loved those parakeets? We wandered around our neighborhood searching for her lost birds but never found them.

Later that week Mom came home with two beautiful grey love birds. I sat silently, watching as Mom clipped their wings with the huge stainless steel pinking shears she used for her upholstery hobby. I wondered how she could do that to the birds, practically cutting their entire wings off both sides.

Suddenly I blurted out, "Mom, doesn't it hurt the birds?"

"No," she said. "They can't feel a thing. I don't want any more birds escaping!"

I had often felt like that: Wanting to spread my own wings by escaping faraway to college, away from the stress at home, since I often had to be a parent to my three younger siblings while my parents were away.

I vowed to never let anyone clip my wings!

I applied to colleges, worked hard, and saved money to move to Los Angeles to become a TV broadcaster and make a difference in the world. I secretly applied to the college of my dreams and, when the acceptance letter arrived, I sat at the dinner table and announced the good news. My dad was so upset that he threw his glass right at me! I ducked and, shattering on the wall behind, the glass' wine splattered on the glass window, showering my siblings and me with red droplets.

For the next four years, I paid for college alone by working eighteen-hour days, two full-time jobs each summer, and one during the school year. After graduating with honors, my beaming parents and my siblings in the audience, I was ready to soar like an eagle.

Following just a few months of working at my dream job as a producer at KNBC-TV, I realized it was not for me.

I later competed in a scholarship pageant, earning the title of Ms. Santa Monica and a $500 cashprize. The best prize, however, came in the form of a new career I never expected: I won a line of Mary Kay products and joined Mary Kay Inc. My mentor Mary Kay Ash was a pioneer in enriching women's lives by teaching financial independence and living her motto of faith first, family second, and career third.

I appreciated those values.

I phased out my career in journalism and for the next twenty-three years I worked to help women strengthen their wings; teaching them how to fly in their own successful businesses. Together our unit, Denise's Dancing Eagles, earned dozens of career cars and my children all came home from the hospital in the famous pink Cadillac. I was living my passion and soaring like an eagle.

However, my husband, a handsome and successful executive who sold private jets, was not doing so well. After a decade of marriage, two beautiful children, and a fairytale jet-set lifestyle, his dad died of Lou Gehrig's disease. Watching his father slowly die, he became depressed and dependent on prescription drugs and alcohol. He had quit his job, and often talked about not wanting to live. I didn't tell anyone, continuing to try to keep it all together, often wondering how I let my life get so out of control.

My children and I had endured years of verbal abuse and there was a lot of fighting. I had tried to control his drinking by covering it up. Lying to my kids, saying, "Daddy is just really tired," as they watched me struggle to pick him up at the bottom of the stairs he had just tumbled down. I finally realized it was time to tell the truth.

Years of prayers and counseling didn't work either. It was nearing the end of my marriage, yet I had no idea how to start anew! *Who would help me?* I was a caged bird with two broken wings. On the outside everything looked wonderful, but on the inside I had crashed and burned. I needed a miracle, or an angel. *Who would believe what was really happening in our home?* I lived in shame, not yet having the guts to stand up for myself and my children by leaving. I worked harder to save money and became more resentful that my husband wasn't working. I gave ultimatums. I told my husband that if he wouldn't stop drinking, I wanted to divorce immediately.

Just when my life couldn't get any more confusing, a few short weeks later, I realized I was pregnant with our third daughter. Our older children were then eight and ten. *What was God thinking?* Is this a sign that I should stay in this marriage? I cried out, "No, God! No! This isn't safe for my kids. We can't stay!"

Within hours, I rushed to LAX, hopped on an airplane and flew to San Jose. I needed to have a talk with my dad.

"Daddy, I need you to listen and not interrupt until I'm finished," I shared the saga of my broken dreams. Three hours later, my dad had the whole story of the marriage I had shamefully hidden. Nothing but the truth. "Daddy, I am planning to get divorced and I think I may be pregnant. I don't think I can go through this alone. I don't want to lose the two men I've loved most in my life. I feel so alone and don't know what to do," I told him, sobbing hysterically.

I stared at him with bloodshot eyes. "OK. You can talk now, Daddy."

He could have washed his hands off his eldest daughter, like he did when I went away to college. Instead, with tears rolling down his cheeks, he predicted, "Denise, someday, that baby you are carrying will be your very best friend. It's an angel. There's a reason that baby is coming now. You don't see it yet, but you will. You have my support and we are a team. We will get through this as a family."

I filed for divorce. We agreed on 50/50 custody. Restraining orders were filed. "Neither party shall drink for twelve hours prior to their custodial time with the children." He got the odd days and I got the even ones. I was growing out my clipped wings, one day at a time!

I was on total bed rest for the final trimester of my high-risk pregnancy. While we lived in the same house the entire pregnancy, my estranged husband rarely spoke to me. I bought my first laptop computer and orchestrated my Mary Kay beauty consultants from my bed. My daughter really was an angel, her pending arrival giving me daily strength and courage. Angels know how to fly. I decided to call her Angel. I was a one-winged angel – the other wing having been totally crushed – and when my baby comes along, I thought, she will embrace me with her love. Together we would keep an eye on the sky and fly.

Nine months later, my brothers and sister helped me pack up my pink Cadillac, two u-haul trucks, and along with my two kids and Golden Retriever, we moved into our new home. Exactly two weeks later, our little Angel was born. After witnessing the birth, my starstruck eleven year-old daughter looked into my eyes, smiling. She then leaned down, and managing the huge scissors alone, she was privileged to cut Angel's umbilical cord.

In our new home we were content and to this day my dad remains my biggest cheerleader. I raised Angel alone until she was nearly three years old. In 2007, a contentious custody battle commenced over Angel, who now lives 50% of the time with her father. My faith and family carried me through it all.

After five years of living alone with my children, I decided to date again, and in 2009 I remarried. This time, I was going to make sure it was someone that didn't have a drinking problem. As we took our vows, I examined the church's marble altar, carved with a mama bird wrapping her strong wings around her three young fledglings.

It was very symbolic for me.

Shortly after the fairy tale wedding, my new husband exhibited a mental health illness that I didn't even know existed. Just weeks into our marriage, things turned violent and I felt again like a trapped bird with battered wings. This husband, who had rarely put alcohol to his lips in the two years we dated long distance, suddenly started drinking an entire bottle of wine right out of the bottle! His eyes would rage and his out-of-control devilish spirit would start throwing things around the house. One day, he tore our entire house apart, breaking doors and window screens and shattering glass picture frames.

This was not safe for my children, and I prayed, "God, I need a sign!" The sign came from heaven in the form of a beautiful monarch butterfly. It was floating around my patio, fluttering its wings and peeking at me through the sliding door. I rushed outside with my arms spread wide open and started dancing with that butterfly. Just then, a song came blaring on my stereo, Martina McBride's *In My Daughter's Eyes*.

"In my daughter's eyes, I am a hero,
I am strong and wise, and I know no fear…"

What the heck am I going to do now?

My counselor had recommended an immediate divorce: You are not safe with this man. Your children are at risk. This is one of the most difficult mental illnesses to treat. In fact, it's almost untreatable. I suggest getting him out of the house, changing the locks on your doors and all your phone numbers, or he will continue to stalk you. It has to be over," warned my counselor.

"No way!" I screamed! "I just got married."

"But the truth is plain to see,
She was sent to rescue me."

I remembered what my dad had said: that my baby would be my best friend and that God had brought her into the world to rescue me to stand up for what was right. "We are a family."

"In my daughter's eyes,
… Darkness turns to light,
And the world is at peace,
This miracle God gave to me,
Gives me strength when I am weak,
It's hanging on when your heart has had enough,
It's giving more when you feel like giving up,
I've seen the light,
It's in my daughter's eyes."

Keep hanging on. I am strong and wise. I will survive. I tried to keep the marriage together, committed to making it work.

Just a few days later, however, my husband tried to kill himself in our home. I had no more options. I wanted to stay alive. I had to end our short marriage. I had my faith, my family, and a lot more experience this time. *The kids and I would be OK.*

Exactly one year after I took my vows on the altar, I was at a women's retreat in my church, staring at the exact same altar with the nest and the baby birds emblazoned on it, arguing with God about how my life could have gotten so messed up. Maybe divorce was the right thing to do in my counselor's and daughters' eyes, but what about God's eyes?

Had I made the right choice? Everything seemed hopeless.

"Please God, show me the way. I refuse to be a caged bird, but now both of my wings are broken. Will I ever fly freely again?" I pleaded. Then, I heard my answer.

It came loudly over the soft murmur of guitar music floating throughout the church. God's words thundered into my heart: "Today, you will start Wings of Love."

I looked around at the many priests taking confession, and the others in the church. *Did anyone else hear that?* No, it was just me. God gave me courage to escape my cage. I knew God's will and I had my miracle. My Angel and my other two children.

The struggle was over. We were safe.

We were free to fly. I knew God would carry us.

Bandaging my broken wings once again, I took my mission from God and founded Wings of Love

Together we can soar.

About the Author

Denise O'Brien, a charismatic and passionate author, businesswoman, international public speaker, and philanthropist inspires others to live their dreams. Her integrity and tenacity have contributed to six successful businesses in marketing, advertising, publishing, event planning, beauty and fashion, and non-profit management.

A single mother, Denise is the founder & CEO of Wings of Love International, Inc., an international non-profit organization serving domestic abuse survivors. WINGS mission is to empower, educate, and inspire a pathway from abuse to emotional health, wholeness, and abundance.

She is the international president of the Ufunguo Community Development Project in Kenya,a member of the International Panel of The Global Film, Fashion, Music, Television, Theatre and Sports Awards, and CEO of DOME Consulting.

In 2012 Denise was recognized with the Loyola Marymount University Social Entrepreneur of the Year Award, and she is ranked in the top 1% of Mary Kay Inc., prioritizing her life with her faith first, her family second, and her career third.

http://www.denise-obrien.com

THE ATTITUDE OF GRATITUDE

Sharon Rogers

I should have realized much earlier in my life that I was destined to help others achieve the life of their dreams. I've always been the one that others have come to with their problems, in search of life's answers. But I never felt I had the solutions these beautiful souls needed... until now.

It all started when I left university after only one month of my business law course. Head held low, I came back home to live with Mum, Dad, and my five brothers and sisters in country Victoria, Australia. Many events followed as I asked God and the Universe to guide me to where I needed to go, and the answer came clearly: to help business people by working at our local radio station, 3SH.

I loved the contact I had with these wonderfully enthusiastic people who allowed me into their lives. I was employed to sell radio advertizing to these business owners, but 90% of my job in reality was listening to their worries and dreams. Yet I didn't feel well equipped to help them solve their worries.

Since then, I have become a life coach and feel I am living the divine design of my life and have finally found my life's purpose. I can't personally solve my clients' problems, but I can help them on a path to achieve their dream goals so that they focus on bringing positive experiences into their lives and into the lives of all they meet.

Through trial and error I have learnt that being grateful is the secret to living the life of your dreams; to unleashing your unlimited potential. Being grateful every day for the wonderful things and people you have in your life sets you on the frequency to achieving your dreams. Being thankful for the sun that rises every morning to warm the earth, for the hot water we shower under, for that which we walk on, for the reliable car we drive, and for the food we eat: it all gives you a head start in fulfilling your dreams!

So many wonderful things have happened in my life since I have used gratitude in my everyday life. I have married an amazing man who is a wonderful father to our two beautiful boys. I have given birth to two healthy and energetic boys who have taught me so much about being patient, caring, and tolerant. Additionally, I have set up a successful fitness business focusing on running water-aerobics classes which has helped people lose weight, increase their health and flexibility, and overcome mental health issues. I have also ran half-marathon fun runs and, last but not least, have set up a successful and rewarding life-coaching business where I work with mothers who want to live a life of purpose and prosperity to achieve the divine design of their lives. And so much more!

The attitude of gratitude is my motivation to living the most wonderful and amazing life, and this is what I want for you to experience. What are you waiting for? Realize your full potential right now! I strongly suggest that you start a gratitude journal, if you haven't already done so.

I have been very privileged to have met many wonderful people and come across many amazing products to assist me on my journey of living a life of purpose and prosperity through motherhood. I understand the pressures we put on ourselves as mothers who want to live a life of purpose and prosperity, and at the same time, care for our family, home, and work, whether part-time or full-time. We also pressure ourselves with ferrying our children to after-school activities, putting up with the emotional roller coaster of school life and with being a supportive and caring partner as well.

We are really trying to attract abundance in all areas of our life so that we can stop feeling so pressured to be super woman! I have found a simple solution to attracting this beautiful abundance into our lives, with the abundance stone set.

These four beautiful stones are:

- Citrine: to inspire your creative drive.

- Jade: helps promote wisdom, fidelity, confidence, and self-sufficiency.

- Smokey Quartz: keeps your visions grounded.

- Clear Quartz: charges and amplifies your manifestations.

I have found that when you carry these stones with you during the day and even put them under your pillow at night, the stones help attract messages of wisdom to help you alleviate your situation.

I also understand now how strong our bond is with our children, that sometimes stress and worry take over our lives. We seem to worry about every little detail going on with their lives: are they warm enough? Cool enough? In safe hands with the babysitter? Are they being bullied or are they bullying? Are they listening to their teacher? Do they exhibit normal behavior at school? Are they concentrating? Up to their grade standard?

Sometimes we just need some help to alleviate these stresses and anxieties and I have found the perfect anxiety and stress relief stone set.

These four beautiful stones are:

- Lepidolite: connects you to the present.

- Red Jasper: balances and calms your emotional body.

- Blue Calcite: helps you detach from external energies.

- Sunstone: relieves your fears and elevates your mood.

As with the abundance stone set, I have found that when you carry these stones with you during the day and even keep them under your pillow at night, the stones help calm your mind and body, and they also attract messages of wisdom to help you alleviate your situation.

The 40-Day Prosperity Plan

This remarkable program assisted me to create positive energy so I could raise my vibration to attract an abundance of wealth, health, love, and self-expression into my life and the lives of my family members. All I had to do to see amazing things happen was to meditate on ten very unique paragraphs once a day for forty days. Some examples of what happened during this time were my taxes from four years before being paid to me unexpectedly, more paying clients coming to my water aerobics classes, health issues being resolved immediately, and much more.

We all want to live a life of purpose and passion, so this is why I have told you about everything that has helped me to live this way. It is never too late to be an amazing mother and live a life of purpose and prosperity.

About the Author

Sharon Rogers is a well-known life coach who specializes in mentoring mothers who want to live a life of purpose and prosperity. She uses the principles of the Law of Attraction and the attitude of gratitude to help her clients achieve the life of their dreams. Sharon is the author of *8 Steps to Living the Life of Your Dreams*.

http://www.lifechangingsuccesscoaching.com

SHARE YOUR STORY AND JOIN THE COMMUNITY

Have a Story to Share?

Everyone has a story, including you! With several *Adventures in Manifesting* titles in production each year, we are constantly looking for more journeys to share. Ask yourself, *what story of mine could change someone's life?*

Whether you have a story to tell or lesson to teach, we're listening. Share yours and get the guide to writing and submitting your chapter here:

www.AdventuresInManifesting.org

The stories we keep an eye out for are any that has to do with manifesting (success, spirituality, health, happiness, wealth, love prosperity, inner guidance, achieving dreams, overcoming obstacles, etc.).

If chosen as a top submission, we will get in touch directly to invite you to be a part of one of our next *Adventures in Manifesting* titles.

Looking for Guidance?

AdventuresInManifesting.org is also a place to freely join a course & community with lessons and action guides for manifesting.

By training you to develop rituals for success and creating the space to get the energy flowing, it will enable you to focus on your intentions from the purest place possible.

www.AdventuresInManifesting.org

Join now to surround yourself with some incredible individuals. It truly is a place of joyful intention marked with the loving energy of gratitude and appreciation.

Feeling Inspired?

We always love to hear how our readers were touched, inspired or changed by the stories shared. If you'd like to share your experience, then you guessed it, hop on over to the AdventuresInManifesting.org home page to let us know!

MORE ADVENTURES IN MANIFESTING TITLES

--iBooks and Kindle--

All Älska titles can be found through the www.AdventuresInMani-festing.org portal or requested from your local bookstore (and found through online bookstores as well).

Books

Adventures in Manifesting: Success and Spirituality

Adventures in Manifesting: Health and Happiness

Adventures in Manifesting: Passion and Purpose

Adventures in Manifesting: Healing from Within

Adventures in Manifesting: Love and Oneness

The Kindle and iBooks

Each of the Adventures in Manifesting titles above can also be purchased via the Amazon Kindle or iTunes iBook formats via AdventuresInManifesting.org.

SHARE WITH LOVE

Is someone you know on the deep and profound journey within? If so, be sure to share with them the entire book or specific stories you intuitively felt would resonate with them.

The meaning of Älska is 'to Love' (it's a Swedish Verb!)

The *chapters* were written with Love.

The *book* was published with Love.

And now it's up to you to *share* with Love.

From the bottom of our hearts and deepest depths of our soul, thank you, thank you, thank you.

With Love & Gratitude,

Älska

http://www.AlskaPublishing.com